The American Novel series provides students of American literature with introductory critical guides to great works of American literature. Each volume begins with a substantial introduction by a distinguished authority on the text, giving details of the work's composition, publication history, and contemporary reception, as well as a survey of the major critical trends and readings from first publication to the present. This overview is followed by a group of new essays, each specifically commissioned from a leading scholar in the field, which together constitute a forum of interpretative methods and prominent contemporary ideas on the text. There are also helpful guides to further reading. Specifically designed for undergraduates, the series will be a powerful resource for anyone engaged in the critical analysis of major American novels and other important texts.

This book provides a multifaceted introduction to Noble Prize–winner Saul Bellow's most widely read and taught work of fiction, *Seize the Day*. This tragicomic story of one day in the life of an average man on the brink of failure and despair is a prime example of the Jewish novel of the 1950s. The essays in this volume examine the thematic, stylistic, and critical elements of Bellow's masterpiece and offer different approaches to how the novel may or may not be thought of as "ethnic."

Michael P. Kramer is Associate Professor of English at Bar-Ilan University.

★ The American Novel ★

Emory Elliott
University of California, Riverside

Other works in the series:

The Great Gatsby
Adventures of Huckleberry Finn
Moby-Dick
Uncle Tom's Cabin
The Last of the Mohicans
The Red Badge of Courage
The Sun Also Rises
A Farewell to Arms
The American
The Portrait of a Lady
Light in August
The Awakening
Invisible Man
Native Son
Their Eyes Were Watching God
The Grapes of Wrath
Winesburg, Ohio

Sister Carrie
The Rise of Silas Lapham
The Catcher in the Rye
White Noise
The Crying of Lot 49
Walden
Poe's Major Tales
Rabbit, Run
Daisy Miller and The Turn of the Screw
Hawthorne's Major Tales
The Sound and the Fury
The Country of the Pointed Firs
Song of Solomon
Wise Blood
Go Tell It on the Mountain
The Education of Henry Adams
Go Down, Moses
Call It Sleep

New Essays on
Seize the Day

Edited by
Michael P. Kramer

CAMBRIDGE
UNIVERSITY PRESS

PUBLISHED BY THE PRESS SYNDICATE OF THE UNIVERSITY OF CAMBRIDGE
The Pitt Building, Trumpington Street, Cambridge CB2 1RP, United Kingdom

CAMBRIDGE UNIVERSITY PRESS
The Edinburgh Building, Cambridge CB2 2RU, UK   http://www.cup.cam.ac.uk
40 West 20th Street, New York, NY 10011-4211, USA   http://www.cup.org
10 Stamford Road, Oakleigh, Melbourne 3166, Australia

First published 1998

Printed in the United States of America

Typeset in Meridien 10/13 pt in Quark XPress™ [BV]

*A catalog record for this book is available from
the British Library*

Library of Congress Cataloging-in-Publication Data
New essays on Seize the day / edited by Michael P. Kramer.
p.   cm. – (American novel)
Includes bibliographical references.
ISBN 0-521-55129-3. – ISBN 0-521-55902-2 (pbk.)
1. Bellow, Saul. Seize the day.   2. Failure (Psychology) in
literature.   3. Jews in literature.   I. Kramer, Michael P., 1952–
II. Series.
PS3503.E4488S4   1998
813'.52 – dc21   97-39145

ISBN 0 521 55129 3 hardback
ISBN 0 521 55902 2 paperback

Contents

vii

Contents

5

Yizkor for Six Million:
Mourning the Death of Civilization in
Saul Bellow's *Seize the Day*

6
Death and the Post-Modern Hero/Schlemiel:
An Essay on *Seize the Day*

Series Editor's Preface

In literary criticism the last twenty-five years have been particularly fruitful. Since the rise of the New Criticism in the 1950s, which focused attention of critics and readers upon the text itself – apart from history, biography, and society – there has emerged a wide variety of critical methods which have brought to literary works a rich diversity of perspectives: social, historical, political, psychological, economic, ideological, and philosophical. While attention to the text itself, as taught by the New Critics, remains at the core of contemporary interpretation, the widely shared assumption that works of art generate many different kinds of interpretations has opened up possibilities for new readings and new meanings.

Before this critical revolution, many works of American literature had come to be taken for granted by earlier generations of readers as having an established set of recognized interpretations. There was a sense among many students that the canon was established and that the larger thematic and interpretative issues had been decided. The task of the new reader was to examine the ways in which elements such as structure, style, and imagery contributed to each novel's acknowledged purpose. But recent criticism has brought these old assumptions into question and has thereby generated a wide variety of original, and often quite surprising, interpretations of the classics, as well as of rediscovered works such as Kate Chopin's *The Awakening,* which has only recently entered the canon of works that scholars and critics study and that teachers assign their students.

The aim of The American Novel Series is to provide students of American literature and culture with introductory critical guides to American novels and other important texts now widely read and studied. Usually devoted to a single work, each volume begins with an introduction by the volume editor, a distinguished authority on the text. The introduction presents details of the work's composition, publication history, and contemporary reception, as well as a survey of the major critical trends and readings from first publication to the present. This overview is followed by four or five original essays, specifically commissioned from senior scholars of established reputation and from outstanding younger critics. Each essay presents a distinct point of view, and together they constitute a forum of interpretative methods and of the best contemporary ideas on each text.

It is our hope that these volumes will convey the vitality of current critical work in American literature, generate new insights and excitement for students of American literature, and inspire new respect for and new perspectives upon these major literary texts.

Emory Elliott
University of California, Riverside

Introduction
The Vanishing Jew: On Teaching Bellow's *Seize the Day* as Ethnic Fiction

MICHAEL P. KRAMER

The secular Jew is a figment; when a Jew becomes a secular person he is no longer a Jew. This is especially true for makers of literature.
  – Cynthia Ozick[1]

Even when he succeeds in detaching himself fairly completely from Jewish life, [the Jewish writer] continues to exhibit all of the restless, agonizing rootlessness that is the Jew's birthmark.
  – Irving Howe[2]

This whole Jewish writer business is sheer invention – by the media, by critics and by "scholars."
  – Saul Bellow[3]

A FEW YEARS AGO, visiting at the Hebrew University in Jerusalem, I taught *Seize the Day* in an introductory undergraduate course on "The American Novel." The students, mostly native and immigrant Israeli Jews, had already read a number of "standard" American works – Hawthorne's *The House of the Seven Gables*, Melville's *Moby-Dick*, Howells' *The Rise of Silas Lapham*, Hemingway's *The Sun Also Rises* – and we were closing the course with two "ethnic" texts, Hurston's *Their Eyes Were Watching God* (which we had just finished) and Bellow's short novel. The idea was to acquaint these Israeli students not only with selected works of American fiction but also with the culture of the American academy, to recreate for them the multiculturalist challenge that has invigorated American literary study in recent years, leading us to reformulate canons and, even more important, to re-examine critical assumptions about the relationship between culture and imagination. The strategy for discussing *Seize the Day* was to begin with the series of familiar Americanist oppositions that we had already raised in relation to the other novels – romance and realism, past and present, success and failure, material and spiritual, alienation and commitment, individual and community – and then to proceed to the "Jewish" question, to see if and how it changed our view of the novel.

I have to admit that I recall very little about the first part of the discussion. I suppose it went predictably. No doubt we compared Tommy Wilhelm's spiritual struggle to that of Hemingway's Jake Barnes, his financial fall to that of Howells' Lapham, his "drowning" to that of Melville's Pip. And so on. A lively discussion with a group of bright and interested students, locating Tommy in a history of American literary characters and *Seize the Day* in "the great tradition" of American novels.[4]

But I do remember well what happened when I asked, "Is this a work of ethnic literature? Is this a *Jewish* as well as an American novel?" The students were uniformly, resolutely skeptical. Some even seemed surprised at the question. They knew, to be sure, that Bellow himself was Jewish. They realized as well that all the characters in the story were nominally Jewish – Adler, Rubin, Perls, Rappaport, Tamkin. Most noticed the passing reference to Yom Kippur and caught the few allusions to the Holocaust. And yes, Tommy's grandfather called him by the Yiddish name Velvel. Still, they judged, *Seize the Day* was not a Jewish novel, at least not in the way *Their Eyes Were Watching God* was African American. Hurston plunges the reader into a fictional world in which ethnicity is palpable, a world rich in Black dialect and folkways. But the ethnicity of *Seize the Day* seemed to them at most incidental.

Perhaps I should not have been surprised at the response. After all, most students (and teachers, too) judge the ethnicity of literary works in a straightforward, no-nonsense way. They usually employ two simple criteria. First, the author must belong to the ethnic group in question. Second, the work must display recognizable ethnic content: most important, the ethnic identity of the characters should be clear. Saul Bellow's Jewishness is a genealogical fact. And so, in a fictional sense, is Tommy Wilhelm's. However, Tommy doesn't look Jewish or sound Jewish. He doesn't speak Hebrew or Yiddish. He doesn't eat Jewish food, and he has a non-Jewish girlfriend. (It's unclear whether his wife is Jewish.) He *forgets* Yom Kippur and recalls the Holocaust only in passing. He only vaguely recalls the Jewish prayer for the dead. And he never mentions Israel. The first time a substantive Jewish issue is raised in relation to Tommy – a full two-thirds of the way into the novel, Dr. Tamkin asks him whether he has experienced antisemitism as a traveling salesman – he responds, "I can't afford to notice."[5] A vague sense of longing (or belonging) remains, but one would be pressed even to call it nostalgia. He does not even actively *reject* Judaism. The reason he drops his Jewish family name is not so much to escape Jewishness as a father "who has no religion" (86). "By definition," writes Sam Girgus, and my students would certainly agree, "the ethnic novel dramatizes group identity and connection."[6] But Tommy's Jewishness doesn't even seem to be at issue. It is only – emphatically *only* – a genealogical fact. So from the students' point of view, the novel had no ethnic content. Hence, it could not be considered Jewish.

Yet I was taken aback by the students' reaction. Bellow, after all, is *supposed* to be a Jewish novelist. He's *supposed* to write Jewish fiction. Since his first appearance on the American literary scene in the mid-forties, Bellow has been labeled and celebrated as such. (Much to his chagrin: "People who make labels," he has commented, "should be in the gumming business."[7]) Critic after critic has commented – often with unbridled enthusiasm – on the Jewish influences on Bellow's work, the Jewishness of his characters and settings, of his language, of his thought and vision. Indeed, for many, he is the quintessential Jewish-American novelist. Alfred Kazin, Bellow's contemporary and long-time admirer, assures us that Bellow is "fascinated and held by the texture of Jewish experience," that the fascination "follow[s] from some deep cut in [his] mind," and that he thus "has been able to personify the Jew in all his *mental* existence, to fit ancient preconceptions to our urban landscape, to create the suffering, reaching, grasping, struggling mind of contemporary Jews."[8] L. H. Goldman, co-editor of the *Saul Bellow Journal*, even asks us to believe, not only that "Saul Bellow's perspective is unmistakably Jewish," but that "the philosophy of Judaism is

3

part and parcel of [Bellow's] very being and manifests itself in
the kind of writing he produces.''[9]

Certainly there are other approaches to Bellow's work. Scholars have hardly restricted themselves to questions of Bellow's
Jewishness – as evidenced in this volume by Sam Girgus, a
scholar with impressive Jewish-ist and ethnicist credentials, who
nevertheless contributes an ethnicity-neutral, psycho-cinematic
reading of *Seize the Day*. (Intriguingly, however, Girgus does turn
at the end of his essay to a description of elderly *Jewish* bodies in
''an uptown New York Auschwitz.'') And some who do deal with
the ethnic question – from Maxwell Geismar writing in 1958 to
Emily Budick in these pages – find his Jewishness (such as it is)
neither impressive nor appealing.[10] Still, I found the chasm between critical claims and student perceptions puzzling, to say the
least. How could *Seize the Day* be both ''a powerful Jewish work''
and hardly Jewish at all?[11]

I decided to press the issue of palpable ethnicity, choosing one
of the scenes toward the end of the novella in which Jewishness
is presented clearly and directly. ''What, then,'' I asked, ''do you
make of this passage?'' I picked up my well-thumbed copy of the
book and read aloud:

> But Tamkin was gone. Or rather, it was he himself who was carried
> from the street into the chapel. The pressure ended inside, where it was
> dark and cool. The flow of fan-driven air dried his face, which he wiped
> hard with his handkerchief to stop the slight salt itch. He gave a sigh
> when he heard the organ notes that stirred and breathed from the pipes
> and he saw people in the pews. Men in formal clothes and black Hom-
> burgs strode softly back and forth on the cork floor, up and down the
> center aisle. The white of the stained glass was like mother-of-pearl, the
> blue of the Star of David like velvet ribbon.[12]

Why, I asked, at this crucial, dramatic moment in the narrative,
as Wilhelm is about to undergo *something* – catharsis, revelation,
communion, breakdown – does Bellow insist on placing that Star
of David in full view of hero and reader?

Silence. I noticed the students looking at each other, puzzled.
Had they missed the reference? Were they rethinking their assumptions? Finally, one student raised her hand and said, ''My

book doesn't say that. My last line is different." Murmuring, heads shaking in assent. I asked her to read her version. "The white of the stained glass was like mother-of-pearl, *with the blue of a great star fluid,* like velvet ribbon" (116, emphasis added).

Serendipity. A quick flip to copyright pages, and, in bare outline, a textual history emerged. My edition – the only one I had ever used – contained the original *Partisan Review* version of 1956, theirs, a version "with author's corrections," first published in 1975. Bellow, we discovered, had revised the text of *Seize the Day.* And he had muted the presence of what is arguably the most recognizable and powerful emblem of Jewishness in modern times.

It was *as if* the Star of David had disappeared before our very eyes. At that pedagogic moment it *seemed* that the students' initial impression had been confirmed by literary-historical fact. (Both Hana Wirth-Nesher and Emily Budick offer in their essays in this volume strong, substantive readings of Bellow's revision. I deal here only with impressions and classroom dynamics.) We might try to explain Bellow's modification in simple aesthetic terms – considering Tommy's confused, anxious state of mind at this point in the narrative, the substitution of subtle description for direct naming makes psychological sense – but it nevertheless *seemed* at the moment that when he revised the text Bellow made a not particularly Jewish story even *less* particularly Jewish, less palpably ethnic.

I realize that these students were not typical in their attitudes toward Jewishness, that they were, in the eighteenth-century sense of the term, *interested.* After all, "Jewish" was the fabric out of which the national life of these students was woven – their language, their sense of history, their calendar. *They* could not forget Yom Kippur because, whether or not they personally fast or go to synagogue, the State officially recognizes Yom Kippur as a national holiday: Schools, businesses, public transportation, all shut down. They couldn't help but recall the Holocaust when, every year on Holocaust and Heroism Memorial Day, sirens sound throughout the country and millions of people stand for a moment in solemn silence, mourning the six million dead. Moreover, this was a group of students keenly sensitive to the appearance – and disappearance – of the Star of David. For them, it was not only a religious but a potent political symbol. Most had served under it, in defense of a state whose very existence was an emphatic expression of unembarrassed, uncontingent Jewishness. Whatever their political or religious beliefs, they were (most of them) Jews in a Jewish state. They understood, to be sure, that "Jewish" could have many different meanings, that it could be – that it *was* – a matter of debate, of confrontation: Israeli society is entrenched in a culture war, not against its Arab neighbors but an internecine war, Jew against Jew. Indeed, in Jerusalem in particular, they were confronted daily with many contending versions of "Jewish," religious, cultural, political. But in Israel, all Jews – secular and religious, hawks and doves, Ashkenazi and Sepharadi – identify themselves *deliberately* as Jews. Tommy Wilhelm's secularity was another story, however: His evanescent Jewishness, his attenuated relationship to religious ritual and national fate, just didn't seem Jewish to them in any substantial way. "Jewish" could not be its absence. From an Israeli point of view, Tommy seemed rather to exemplify the antithesis of Jewishness. He was the assimilated American Jew, a familiar, quasi-mythic figure of Jewish demographic studies – disaffected, intermarrying, disappearing. ("There are probably few more assimilated Jewish characters in American literature," writes Emily Budick, "than Tommy Wilhelm.") He was Jewishly, to borrow Cynthia Ozick's term, a "figment." The disappearance of the Star of David seemed to symbolize for them the sociological phenomenon of the vanishing American Jew.[13]

To ask Israeli Jews to evaluate the Jewishness of a fictional American character or author is to risk blurring the distinction between nationality and ethnicity. The truth is, however, that student reactions to *Seize the Day* are similarly skeptical in the United States. In California, students have wondered about, and even challenged, my inclusion of the novel in courses on Jewish-American literature, not because they share the Israeli sense of Jewishness, but because they also believe that ethnicity should be palpable. In our multiculturalist times, we tend to prefer our ethnic fare well-seasoned with definitive markers of cultural difference: the ghetto, the barrio, the reservation; Yiddish, Spanish,

Black English; a yarmulke, a kimono; klezmer, jazz, salsa; knishes, black-eyed peas, fried rice – markers that distinguish ethnic characters from their nonethnic "American" compatriots. We read ethnic literature, we have revised our canons, because we recognize, respect, and value the differences among peoples. We *expect* group differences and want them to be clearly manifest in the texts produced by group members. Why else study ethnic literature *as* ethnic literature? So when those expectations are not met, we are frustrated, perhaps a bit offended. And *Seize the Day* seems to offer very little of these sorts of otherness. Bellow does not cater to these tastes.

Indeed, he actively discourages them, both in general and, especially, in regard to himself. He bemoans the "ethnic protectionism" of the contemporary academy, regarding it as inhibiting freedom of thought and constraining freedom of expression. (He has written an adulatory preface to Allan Bloom's controversial, anti-multiculturalist critique of the academy, *The Closing of the American Mind*.) And he has always been rather edgy about being considered a Jewish writer, calling the label "an implied put down."[14] Not that he denies or belittles either cultural differences or the *fact* of his Jewishness. "I'm well aware," he has announced time and again, "of being Jewish."[15] He claims that he is painfully conscious of what that identity brings with it, particularly in the twentieth century. "Many have tried to rid themselves in one way or another of this dreadful historic load, by assimilation or other means," he has said, "but I myself have not been tempted."[16] Still, he refuses to accept ethnicity as a sufficient definition. His soul, he has written, "does not feel comfortably accommodated" in "the Jewish-writer category." To be sure, most of his characters, as in *Seize the Day*, are at least nominally Jewish, and many others, as in *Herzog* (1964) and "The Old System" (1967), more palpably so. He has written one book explicitly concerning antisemitism (*The Victim*, 1947) and one about the Holocaust (*Mr. Sammler's Planet*, 1970). He has translated stories from Yiddish (Sholom Aleichem's "Eternal Life" and Isaac Bashevis Singer's "Gimpel the Fool," both 1953) and edited *Great Jewish Short Stories* (1963). He has written journalistic accounts of the Six Day War and of the Begin-Sadat peace treaty and has published a book-length memoir of one of his stays in Israel (*To Jerusalem and Back*, 1976). He accepted the Bnai Brith Jewish Heritage Award in 1968 (as well as the Anti-Defamation League's "America's Democratic Legacy" Award in 1976). Yet, although he claims never to have betrayed his history, he asserts adamantly that he has "never consciously written as a Jew," that he writes only as Saul Bellow, "a person of Jewish origin – American and Jewish – who has had a certain experience of life, which is in part Jewish," but also American, Russian, son-of-immigrants, male, twentieth-century, Midwestern, hockey-fan, and so on. "I simply must deal with the facts of my life – as a basic set of primitive facts. They're my given."[17]

His given, not his goal; his point of origin, not his purpose. In part, Bellow's rejection of the "Jewish writer" label stems from the perception that the American Jewish community was trying to enlist him in its cause. "Since the holocaust," he explains, "[Jews] have become exceptionally sensitive to the image the world has of them" and they "feel that the business of a Jewish writer in America is to write public relations releases, to publicize everything that is nice in the Jewish community and to suppress the rest, loyally."[18] Indeed, he writes, some "Jewish writers [have] bent over backwards just because there was this pressure put on them." But Bellow has determinedly resisted the pressure. He would not, he says, sacrifice artistic integrity in the name of "public relations." He would not agree to produce deliberately "a pleasing impression of Jewish life."[19] He would not, as we say nowadays, be politically correct. "In that respect," he concludes, "I was a great disappointment to them."[20] He sees these sorts of restrictions on literature as of a piece with the programmatic demands that totalitarian regimes make on their writers. A novelist, he argues, cannot be a writer and a propagandist, too. He cannot begin with an explicit political purpose – even a wholly laudable one – and remain true to his art. "If a novelist is going to affirm anything," Bellow writes, "he must be prepared to prove his case in close detail, reconcile it with hard facts." And since "facts are stubborn and refractory," the writer "must even be prepared for the humiliation of discovering that he may have to affirm something different." In other words, for

Bellow, "the art of the novel itself has a tendency to oppose the conscious or ideological purposes of the writer, occasionally ruining the most constructive intentions."[21] If to be a Jewish writer means to write *for* the Jewish community, then "Jewish writer" is a contradiction in terms: A true writer, committed to his art, cannot *by definition* be a Jewish writer in this sense. He cannot be defined by his roots. True literature cannot be ethnic literature. Literature may be (must be) grounded in ethnic detail, for "there is no such a thing as a generalized human being." And "if we dismiss the life that is waiting for us at birth, we will find ourselves in a void." But great writing transcends its own ethnicity. It aspires toward universal truth. And so Bellow has declared: "I don't have any sense of ethnic responsibility. That is not my primary obligation. My primary obligation is to my trade and not to any particular ethnic group."[22]

For Bellow, the spiritual autonomy of the individual is the highest moral good, and he thus sees the writer's goal as giving "new eyes to human beings, inducing them to view the world differently, converting them from fixed modes of experience." So the writer must himself maintain a fiercely independent consciousness "which has the strength to be immune to the noise of history and the distractions of our immediate surroundings."[23] Bellow insists, accordingly, that the "primitive facts" of his life, the various and variegated social and cultural influences he acknowledges, even when viewed in all their complexity and multiplicity, cannot account for the man Saul Bellow. And, most important, they have not impinged on his autonomy as a writer. Hence his declaration: "This whole Jewish writer business is sheer invention." To be a Jewish writer – to be any category of writer – is to be something less than a writer, something less than free. To resist categorization is thus, for Bellow, a matter of principle. "The commonest teaching of the civilized world in our time can be stated simply," he has recently written: " 'Tell me where you come from and I will tell you what you are.' " Bellow sees this teaching – including its current multiculturalist version – not so much as an untruth as an evil, a force to be opposed. For he recognizes that we *can* allow ourselves to be determined by our environments, and Bellow would not allow himself to be so diminished: "I recognized at an early age that I was called upon to decide for myself to what extent my Jewish origins, my surroundings (the accidental circumstances of Chicago), my schooling, were to be allowed to determine the course of my life. I did not intend to be wholly dependent on history and culture. Full dependency must mean that I was done for. . . . Before I was capable of thinking clearly, my resistance to its material weight took the form of obstinacy."[24] Although "I was born into an orthodox family," he writes, "I detested orthodoxy from the first."[25]

Consider, in light of these statements, the following autobiographical account of his early years written in 1955:

My parents emigrated to Canada from Russia in 1913 – my father, a businessman, has often told me that he imported Egyptian onions into St. Petersburg – and settled in the town of Lachine, Quebec. I was born there in 1915, the youngest of four children. Until I was nine years old we lived in one of the poorest and most ancient districts of Montreal, on the slope of St. Dominick Street between the General Hospital and Rachel Market.

In 1924 we moved to Chicago. I grew up there and consider myself a Chicagoan, out and out. Educated after a fashion in the Chicago schools, I entered the University of Chicago in 1933. . . . [T]he university was, for me, a terrifying place. The dense atmosphere of learning, of cultural effort, heavily oppressed me; I felt that wisdom and culture were immense and that I was hopelessly small. In 1935 I transferred to Northwestern University. Northwestern had less prestige, but my teachers there appreciated me more. And of course I wanted to be appreciated. My intelligence revived somewhat and I graduated with honors in anthropology and sociology in 1937.

Graduate school didn't suit me, however. I had a scholarship at the University of Wisconsin, and I behaved very badly. During the Christmas vacation, having fallen in love, I got married and never returned to the University. In my innocence, I had decided to become a writer.[26]

Elsewhere, and at some length in recent years, Bellow has spoken more freely of his early Jewish family life, of his having begun Hebrew study "at about four," of reading the Bible and internalizing the stories of the Patriarchs, of his mother's wanting him to be (if not a fiddler) a rabbi, of family debates over assimilation, and of having it "driven home quite early" that he was "*un juif.*"²⁷ It was important for his development as a writer, he has stated, "that at a most susceptible time of my life I was wholly Jewish," a circumstance he describes as "a gift, a piece of good fortune, with which one doesn't quarrel."²⁸ But in writing a year before the publication of *Seize the Day*, this information, beyond the nonspecific reference to Russian immigrant parents, is suppressed, as if it were inessential. What he does offer is a quasi-picaresque narrative of transfers and displacements: His father imports onions from Egypt to Russia; his parents emigrate from Russia to Canada; the family is uprooted from Montreal to Chicago; he flees the University of Chicago for Northwestern; he leaves graduate school to become a writer. He may very well consider himself a Chicagoan, but only in the most unsettled, peripatetic, Augie-March-like sense, a Chicagoan who is continually, if I may put a twist on the phrase, "out and out." "There was not a chance in the world," Bellow would later remark, "that Chicago . . . would make me in its image."²⁹ And there was certainly no chance, in Bellow's terms, that being "wholly Jewish," however valuable, could accomplish what Chicago could not – not, that is, unless being Jewish meant, in essence, nothing more than being displaced. (More on this possibility later.)

Critics are not obliged to respect authors' pronouncements concerning their own work – certainly not in the face of compelling textual evidence to the contrary. But given my students' judgment of *Seize the Day*, Bellow's resistance to the "Jewish" label struck me as something to be taken seriously. By the same token, neither could the critical insistence on Bellow's Jewishness be ignored. Had the critics detected something my students failed to see – and that Bellow wants us to overlook? Some Jewish-ist critics do acknowledge what my students claim, that *Seize the Day* doesn't seem particularly Jewish, at least not on the surface. They insist, however, that the novel is more Jewish than it seems, that Bellow's Jewishness is deliberately encoded or *malgre lui* embedded in the text. Lillian Kremer, for instance, alert to certain of Bellow's name choices, claims that the novel deals "on an allusive plane" with "the historic antagonism between Hasidim and their Jewish opponents," an esoteric controversy Bellow

(if she is correct) would had to have known in detail.[30] And
L. H. Goldman ambitiously combs through Bellow's prose to un-
cover biblical parallels (particularly the story of Jacob and Esau)
and echoes of classic Rabbinic texts (the Talmud, the Midrash,
the Zohar), as if the Jewish writer, despite his mixed feelings
about his Jewish roots, could not help but think Jewishly.[31] At
its very best – as when Hana Wirth-Nesher reads Bellow's ''translations'' from Hebrew and Yiddish intertextually or Emily Budick
discerns the novel's silent inscriptions of the Holocaust – this sort
of exegesis does not so much discover a hidden Bellow as revise
and enrich our contextual understanding of the author's art and
ethnicity. It can, however, leave us even more befuddled, won-
dering why an author so consciously resistant to the Jewish label
would nevertheless bury such a treasure chest of Jewish knowledge so deeply within his prose.

Most critics, though, do not rely on critical archaeology to
define Bellow's Jewishness. To many, particularly those of the
author's own generation – Alfred Kazin, Leslie Fiedler, Irving
Howe, Jules Chametzky, and others, prominent critics whose relation to the Jewish immigrant experience more or less parallels
his – the ethnicity of *Seize the Day* is not subterranean, not even
implicit, but as palpable and apparent as that of *Their Eyes Were
Watching God*. They find it in the urban setting, in the characters,
and above all in Bellow's language and style, in what Howe describes as a ''mingling of high-flown intellectual bravado with
racy-tough street Jewishness, all in a comic rhetoric that keeps
turning its head back towards Yiddish even as it keeps racing
away from it.''[32] Recalling his own coming to ethnic self-
consciousness in the fifties, cultural historian and editor Ronald
Sanders describes the excitement for him and for his Jewish
friends of reading Bellow and discovering in his prose ''the be-
ginnings of that unique American-Jewish diction, highbrow yet
sidewalk-salty, that was to become a trademark of his and that
seemed to reflect so well on our own patterns of thought and
speech.''[33] Chametzky has even argued that Bellow's development of his characteristic *ethnic* diction is the aesthetic culmina-
tion of the history of the American Jewish novel: it is consequently through this diction that, in the essay that forms a

12

reflective coda to this volume, Chametzky has chosen to recall the cultural and political milieu of the 1950s and, from the informed perspective of four decades, to engage *Seize the Day* in critical conversation.[34]

For Howe, Sanders, Chametzky and the others, Bellow's prose embodies a distinctive, concrete ethnic experience, *their* experience as second-generation Americans. It was an experience – and a prose – characterized by the remarkably successful acculturation of Jews from more or less traditional East European backgrounds into the cultural and intellectual world of modern America. By 1956 Bellow cut an impressive figure in this world. *The Adventures of Augie March* had won him the National Book Award in 1954, and "with the publication of *Seize the Day* [he became] not merely a writer with whom it [was] possible to come to terms, but one with whom it [was] *necessary* to come to terms." (He would win the National Book Award twice more, for *Herzog* in 1964 and for *Mr. Sammler's Planet* in 1970, along with the Pulitzer Prize for *Humboldt's Gift* in 1975 and the Nobel Prize for Literature in 1976.) Clearly, he had "fulfill[ed] the often frustrated attempts [of Jewish writers] to possess the American imagination and to enter the American cultural scene."[35] So Leslie Fiedler judged in 1957, the year after the publication of *Seize the Day*. And many others concurred. Bellow was viewed as representative – for some as the apotheosis – of "a large and impressively gifted group of serious American-Jewish writers [who had] broken through" – were then just breaking through – "the psychic barriers of the past to become an important, possibly a major reformative influence in American life and letters."[36] ("The first generation fled the ghetto or the Pale," wrote Daniel Bell, "the second fled the past itself."[37]) The Jewish experience ascribed to Bellow was, in effect, an experience of Jewishness *as* Americanization, in which the sons – the writers and critics were predominantly male – watched from a cultural distance as the world of their fathers and mothers became less relevant to them and, as it were, vanished. (The cultural significance of Bellow's fictional representation of generational conflict is the subject of Donald Weber's contribution to this collection.) Breakthrough meant, in Chametzky's words, "the Jewish writer's liberation from his

[Jewish] material.''[38] If indeed, as it has been argued, Bellow ''had deeper insight into, and knowledge of, Jewish cultural values than any other major Jewish writer of his time,'' that had to mean as well, Howe explains, ''that he [knew] enough to surmise the extent of our dispossession.''[39]

The Jewishness the critics saw in Bellow – and saw reflected in his writings – was a mirror image of their own. They recognized it, they *felt* it, in everything Bellow wrote. Here was ''a new hero of thought,'' as Sam Girgus has called him, *their* hero, the fictional incarnation of a generation of secular American Jewish intellectuals.[40] (Although Tommy Wilhelm was not strictly speaking an intellectual, they saw themselves, their Jewishness, in him, too.) By 1957, when Norman Podhoretz painted the following composite portrait, the secular Jewish intellectual already formed a clearly perceivable type:

His age is between thirty-five and fifty, which is to say that the experience of the '30's, and involvement with radical politics in one form or another, was a decisive influence in shaping his mind. He was born of immigrant parents from Eastern Europe who were primarily Yiddish-speaking but not particularly observant. His Jewish education was scanty, and there was nothing either in Judaism as he knew it or in the Jewish life around him that exerted any charm over his imagination. . . . [T]he intellectual never denied that he was a Jew [but] made a moral decision not to be cabbinn'd, cribb'd, confined by his Jewishness; he wanted something bigger and nobler, he wanted to be a man of broad cultivation and wide sympathies, whereas Jews struck him as narrow and mean and concerned with no other fate than their own . . . . It was a principled refusal by the young intellectual to allow his character to be determined by conditions, conditions that threatened to warp his best qualities and poison his finest aspirations, conditions that he knew had not been ordained by Providence.[41]

All this, as we have seen, is more or less true of Bellow, more or less how, over the years, he has described himself. Indeed, Podhoretz is merely echoing how, in essay after essay for at least a decade, the intellectuals had been self-consciously describing themselves. ''Our special type,'' wrote Irving Howe in what is perhaps the prototype of these essays, ''is the young American Jew'' who was ''born into an immigrant Jewish family'' and ''has largely lost his sense of Jewishness, of belonging to a people with a meaningful tradition.'' But whereas Podhoretz condemns the intellectual's self-alienation from Jews and Jewishness as a form of self-delusion and self-hatred, Howe sees the phenomenon paradoxically as a powerful *expression* of Jewishness. Although he "cannot, even if he wished to, return to a world no longer his," Howe writes, he nevertheless "feels in his flesh the brand of his people," hears "echoes of the[ir] endless trek," and "continues to exhibit all of the restless, agonizing rootlessness that is the Jew's birthmark." His alienation is "the same sense of alienation that besets the Jews as a group," even as it sets him apart from the group. In short, writes Howe, he is "the rootless son of a rootless people."[42]

Such self-conscious, self-perpetuating irony was essential to the construction of Jewish identity among the writers and intellectuals of the postwar generation. It allowed them, as it were, to be Jewish and not Jewish at the same time. It virtually emptied Jewishness of all palpable content (leaving nothing for my students to recognize) and reconstrued it as style.[43] The fundamental fact of Jewish history was, for the intellectuals, exile: The Jews, expelled from their homeland, became wanderers among the nations. They perceived this fact as motif and conceived motif as essence. They read culture as allegory and collapsed history into biography. (Hence, perhaps, the theme of displacement in Bellow's 1955 thumbnail autobiography.) To be a Jew was not to uphold a certain body of laws and traditions, not to share a certain culture, not to return to Palestine, not to live in a community, but to be *personally* in a condition of exile, an outcast, a pariah, even when – especially when – that meant to be outcast from one's own people. For "in their position as social outcasts," Hannah Arendt explained in 1959, "such men reflect[ed] the political status of their entire people."[44] Their plight, wrote Daniel Bell in 1946, "recapitulate[d] the phylogeny of a race."[45] The secular Jewish intellectual, doubly alienated from his people and from society at large, thus became the quintessential Jew.

Isaac Deutscher captured the paradoxical nature of the construction when he dubbed these sorts of figures "non-Jewish Jews." He found their prototype in the Talmud, in the heretic teacher of Rabbi Meir, Elisha ben Avuya, called derogatorily by the Rabbis, ''Akher,'' the ''Other,'' giving the intellectuals' own heresies, ironically, a hoary respectability, the legitimacy of tradition.[46] But they were clearly a modern phenomenon, products of Enlightenment and Emancipation: Arendt attributed the phenomenon to the disappointments of assimilation, disappointments many times magnified when seen through the historical lens of the Holocaust. ''Realizing only too well that they did not enjoy political freedom nor full admission to the life of nations, but that, instead, they had been separated from their own people and lost contact with the simple natural life of the common man,'' she wrote, ''these men yet achieved liberty and popularity by the sheer force of imagination.''[47] They became social critics: ''The alienated Jew, self-conscious of his position,'' Bell explained, ''knows he is irreconcilable, and by his vocation of alienation sits in judgment on the world.''[48] And they became writers: ''People to whom existence has often been a consciously fearful matter, who have lived at the crossroads between the cultures and on the threshold between life and death,'' Alfred Kazin wrote, ''naturally see existence as tension, issue, and drama'' and ''can do nothing with [their experiences] *but* put them into words.''[49]

Baruch Spinoza, Heinrich Heine, Karl Marx, Bernard Lazare, Rosa Luxemburg, Franz Kafka, Leon Trotsky, Sigmund Freud, Simone Weil, Isaac Rosenfeld, Delmore Schwartz, Clement Greenberg, Paul Goodman – and Saul Bellow.[50] These were the pariahs, the alienated intellectuals, the non-Jewish Jews of modernity. Like other Jews, they dwelled ''on the borderlines of various civilizations, religions, and national cultures.'' But unlike more ''Jewish'' Jews, it was held, they were able to ''transcend'' both Judaism and Jewry and translate their marginality into vision, ''to rise in thought above their societies, above their nations, above their times and generations, and to strike out mentally into wide new horizons and far into the future.'' Still, no matter how far they traveled from Judaism, it was argued, these thinkers and writers ''had in themselves something of the quintessence of Jewish life and of the Jewish intellect.''[51] Their vision ultimately ''came from the profound history embedded in

16

Judaism," Kazin wrote, "a vision in which the subtle purposiveness of history always managed to reassert itself in the face of repeated horrors."[52] They formed, it was held, a "hidden tradition" within Judaism, a tradition of rejecting tradition, a counter-history ignored or repressed by official historians of the Jewish people. Yet it was they "who really did most for the spiritual dignity of their people."[53] And standing at the end of this history, were the post-Holocaust generation of secular Jewish intellectuals themselves, the self-appointed spiritual heirs of a Jewish tradition they themselves were inventing, spreading the new, non-Jewish Jewish gospel in America.

They were, by all accounts, remarkably successful, "chang[ing] for all time the atmosphere of American letters."[54] One reason is that they appealed not only to Jews but to non-Jews, transforming themselves and their Jewishness into myth. "Not only the Jews are in *galut* [exile]," they preached.[55] In the modern world, in the shadow of war and genocide, dehumanizing technologies and demoralizing bureaucracies, alienation was touted as the "fundamental experience of our time" and the Jew's "life and his wanderings" were perceived as "the image of the world's destiny."[56] "At one time the experience of exile, of being a victim, lonely, harassed, burdened with a guilt not his own, served to separate the Jew from his fellow man," wrote Harold Fisch. "Now such consciousness has become the common heritage of a whole generation of survivors and 'displaced persons.' "[57] The once-despised Jew was "mythicized into the representative American," which in the postwar period is to say, into the representative man.[58] "Definitely," wrote Alfred Kazin, "it was now the thing to be Jewish."[59] And, in the imaginative world of the intellectuals, everyone could be. "Every man is a Jew," announced Bernard Malamud, "though he may not know it."[60]

For the critics of the postwar generation, Bellow's novels were Jewish precisely because they both embodied and transcended Jewishness. "We recognize the Bellow character," wrote Leslie Fiedler, because as a Jew "he is openly what we [all] are in secret," because he is "the person who, all amenities stripped away, feels himself stripped to his human essence." He is "essential man,'' which meant both ''the Jew in perpetual exile and Huck Finn.''[61] In him, the Jew and American meet and merge. In a sense, then, my students were right: their inability to see the Jewishness of *Seize the Day* can be understood as astute critical commentary upon the socio-historical process of acculturation, a mark, as it were, of Bellow's success. Having offered himself as the model American, the Jew as Bellow and his fellows saw him and valued him *had* virtually vanished, and the removal of the Star of David could be read as a farewell (perhaps unwitting, perhaps not) to ethnic difference. For if the Jew is Everyman and Everyman is the Jew, then ethnic difference rhetorically loses its cultural and spitritual dimension and is effectually reduced to genealogy, to descent – which is to say, strictly speaking, to race.

Of course, both historically and conceptually, race is no negligible matter. Although ''in this century, so agonizing to the Jews'' (to quote Bellow)[62] we may feel impelled to downplay its significance, we nevertheless cannot, as students of ethnicity, do without it. For better or worse, it is the ultimate, *palpable* foundation of all ethnic identification and the starting point of all ethnic imagining. Race is where we begin when we construct syllabi for ethnic literature courses and tables of contents for ethnic studies anthologies. Only after we check an author's genealogical credentials do we even consider including his or her works. Spiritual questions come later. We may fairly judge with my students that the vanishing Jew is *spiritually* hardly a Jew at all. We may demand that, rightfully to be called a Jew, Tommy should be more religious, more culturally literate, more politically committed. Indeed, that's exactly what Tommy himself does when he internalizes his father's conviction that he is ''the wrong kind of Jew'' (86). Such judgments can (and often do) have compelling polemical and even moral force, but they do not change the fact that the ''wrong kind of Jew'' is, by definition, a Jew for all that – if nothing else, still a Jew ''according to the flesh.''[63]

To teach *Seize the Day* as ethnic fiction, we must thus begin with the genealogical fact of Bellow's Jewishness. What Bellow made of the ''stubborn and refractory'' fact – the affirmations and denials, the essays and, above all, the fiction – are the raw materials of literary and intellectual history. What we, critics, teachers, and students, make of the imaginative consequences of the fact is the substance of ethnic (and in particular, Jewish) literary studies. On its authority we may locate *Seize the Day* within certain linguistic and literary traditions (Wirth-Nesher), or read the novel as an emotional protest against civility (Weber), or judge it as a manifestation of self-hatred (Budick). We may paint it as a constellation of cultural elements (Chametzky) or recall it only briefly as a simple physical fact (Girgus). We may even construe it as its own negation. Without a racial *fundamentum*, "non-Jewish Jew" is but a contradiction in terms. But as long as he is understood to be a Jew "according to the flesh," an author (or a character) can still be imagined to feel "in his flesh the brand of his people." He can still be conceptualized – despite and through his deracination – as the quintessential Jew. The Star of David doesn't *really* disappear; it only *seems* to.

NOTES

1 Cynthia Ozick, "Toward a New Yiddish," in *Art and Ardor* (New York: Knopf, 1983), p. 169.
2 Irving Howe, "The Lost Young Intellectuals," in Harold U. Ribalow, ed., *Mid-Century: An Anthology of Jewish Life and Culture in Our Times* (New York: The Beechhurst Press, 1955), p. 153.
3 Bellow, in Sanford Pinsker, "Saul Bellow in the Classroom," in *Conversations with Saul Bellow*, eds., Gloria L. Cronin and Ben Siegel (Jackson: University Press of Minnesota, 1994), p. 103.
4 A number of critics see *Seize the Day* in the American grain. See, for example, Richard Chase, "The Adventures of Saul Bellow: Progress of a Novelist," in Irving Malin, ed., *Saul Bellow and the Critics* (New York: New York University Press, 1967), pp. 30–3. Chase is the author of the classic critical work, *The American Novel and its Tradition* (Garden City, New York: Anchor Books, 1957).
5 Saul Bellow, *Seize the Day* (New York: Penguin Books, 1976), p. 81. Unless otherwise indicated, all quotations from *Seize the Day* in this volume will be from this edition and parenthetically noted in the text.
6 Sam Girgus, "The New Ethnic Novel and the American Idea," *College Literature* 20 (1993): 59.

7   Bellow, quoted in Ruth Miller, *Saul Bellow: A Biography of the Imag-
    ination* (New York: St. Martin's Press, 1991), p. 41. For a survey
    of Bellow's comments about his Jewishness and being labeled
    a Jewish writer, see Miller, pp. 39–44. For a selection of essays on
    the subject, see Vinoda and Shiv Kumar, eds., *Saul Bellow: A Sym-
    posium on the Jewish Heritage* (Hyderabad, India: Nachson Books,
    1983).

8   Alfred Kazin, "The Earthly City of the Jews," in *Bright Book of Life:
    American Novelists and Storytellers from Hemingway to Mailer* (Boston:
    Little, Brown,1973), p. 128 (part of the essay appears also in Vi-
    noda and Shiv Kumar, eds., *Saul Bellow: A Symposium on the Jewish
    Heritage*); Kazin, Introduction to Saul Bellow, *Seize the Day*, (New
    York: Fawcett World Library, 1968), pp. viii–ix.

9   L. H. Goldman, "The Jewish Perspective of Saul Bellow," in L. H.
    Goldman, Gloria L. Cronin, and Ada Aharoni, eds., *Saul Bellow: A
    Mosaic* (New York: Peter Lang, 1992), p. 19; Goldman, "Saul Bellow
    and the Philosophy of Judaism," in Gloria L. Cronin and L. H. Gold-
    man, eds., *Saul Bellow in the 1980s: A Collection of Critical Essays* (East
    Lansing: Michigan State University Press, 1989), p. 57.

10 Maxwell Geismar, "Saul Bellow: Novelist of the Intellectuals," re-
    printed in Irving Malin, ed., *Saul Bellow and the Critics* (New York:
    New York University Press, 1967), pp. 10–24.

11 Irving Malin, "The Jewishness of Saul Bellow," *Jewish Heritage*
    (Summer 1964): 54. The essay is reprinted in Vinoda and Shiv
    Kumar, eds., *Saul Bellow: A Symposium on the Jewish Heritage*, pp. 47–
    55.

12 Saul Bellow, *Seize the Day*, introduction by Alfred Kazin (New York:
    Fawcett World Library, 1968), p. 126.

13 Bellow tells the following anecdote: "In Israel, I was often and
    sometimes impatiently asked what sort of Jew I was and how I
    defined myself and explained my existence. I said that I was an
    American, a Jew, a writer by trade. . . . But my Israeli questioners
    or examiners were not satisfied. They were trying to make me
    justify myself. It was their conviction that the life of a Jew in what
    they call the Diaspora must inevitably be 'inauthentic.' " Bellow,
    " 'I Took Myself as I Was . . . ' " *ADL Bulletin* (December 1976): 3.

14 Bellow, quoted in Miller, *Saul Bellow*, p. 43.

15 Bellow, in Sanford Pinsker, ed., "Saul Bellow in the Classroom," p.
    103.

16 Bellow, " 'I Took Myself as I Was . . .'" p. 3.

17 Bellow in Chirantan Kulshrestha, "A Conversation with Saul Bel-

low,'' in *Conversations with Saul Bellow*, pp. 90–1; Bellow, quoted in Miller, *Saul Bellow*, p. 41.

18 Bellow in Kulshrestha, ''A Conversation with Saul Bellow,'' p. 91; Bellow, ''The Swamp of Prosperity,'' *Commentary* 28 (1959): 79. See also Bellow's introduction to *Great Jewish Short Stories* (New York: Dell Books, 1963), pp. 13–14.

19 Bellow, quoted in Miller, *Saul Bellow*, p. 43.

20 Bellow, quoted in Miller, *Saul Bellow*, 43; Bellow in Kulshrestha, ''A Conversation with Saul Bellow,'' p. 91.

21 Bellow, ''The Writer as Moralist,'' *Atlantic Monthly* (March 1963): 60–1.

22 Bellow in Kulshrestha, ''A Conversation with Saul Bellow,'' p. 90; Bellow, '' 'I Took Myself as I Was . . .'', 3; Bellow, quoted in Miller, *Saul Bellow*, p. 42.

23 Bellow, Foreword to Allan Bloom, *The Closing of the American Mind* (New York: Penguin Books, 1987), p. 17.

24 Bellow, Foreword to Bloom, *The Closing of the American Mind*, p. 13.

25 Bellow in Rockwell Gray, et al., ''Interview with Saul Bellow,'' *TriQuarterly* 63 (1985): 650.

26 Bellow, quoted in Stanley J. Kunitz, ed., *Twentieth Century Authors*, 1st Supplement (New York: H. W. Wilson, 1955), p. 72.

27 Bellow, ''A Half Life,'' in *It All Adds Up: From the Dim Past to the Uncertain Future, a Non-Fiction Collection* (London: Secker and Warburg, 1994), pp. 287, 289.

28 Bellow in Kulshrestha, ''A Conversation with Saul Bellow,'' p. 92.

29 Bellow, Foreword to Bloom, *The Closing of the American Mind*, p. 13.

30 S. Lillian Kremer, ''*Seize the Day*: Intimations of Anti-Hasidic Satire,'' *Modern Jewish Studies Annual* and *Yiddish* IV (1982): 32–40.

31 L. H. Goldman, *Saul Bellow's Moral Vision: A Critical Study of the Jewish Experience* (New York: Irvington, 1983), pp. 61–84.

32 Irving Howe, *World of Our Fathers* (New York: Harcourt Brace Jovanovich, 1976), pp. 594–5.

33 Ronald Sanders, ''Ethnicity in the Barracks: Notes Toward Self-Definition,'' *Midstream* 17 (April 1971): 19.

34 See Jules Chametzky, ''The Assimilation of the American Jewish Writer: Abraham Cahan to Saul Bellow,'' in *Our Decentralized Literature: Cultural Mediations in Selected Jewish and Southern Writers* (Amherst: University of Massachusetts Press, 1986), pp. 46–57.

35 Leslie Fiedler, ''Saul Bellow,'' in *To the Gentiles* (New York: Stein and Day, 1972), p. 57. The essay originally appeared in *Prairie*

Schooner, Summer 1957, and was reprinted in Irving Malin, ed., *Saul Bellow and the Critics* (New York: New York University Press, 1967).

36   Irving Malin and Irwin Stark, Introduction to Malin and Stark, eds., *Breakthrough: A Treasury of Contemporary American-Jewish Literature* (Philadelphia: The Jewish Publication Society of America, 1963), p. 1.

37   Daniel Bell, "Reflections on Jewish Identity," *Commentary* 31 (1961): 471.

38   Jules Chametzky, "The Assimilation of the American Jewish Writer," p. 56.

39   Louis Harap, *In the Mainstream: The Jewish Presence in Twentieth Century American Literature, 1950s–1980s* (New York: Greenwood Press, 1987), p. 99; Howe, *World of Our Fathers,* p. 587.

40   Sam Girgus, *The New Covenant: Jewish Writers and the American Idea* (Chapel Hill: University of North Carolina Press, 1984), pp. 3–23.

41   Norman Podhoretz, "The Intellectual and Jewish Fate," *Midstream* 3 (Winter 1957): 16–17. On the cultural and political background of the intellectuals, see Alexander Bloom, *Prodigal Sons: The New York Intellectuals and Their World* (New York: Oxford University Press, 1986); Terry A. Cooney, *The Rise of the New York Intellectuals: Partisan Review and Its Circle* (Madison: University of Wisconsin Press, 1986); Mark Schechner, *After the Revolution: Studies in the Contemporary Jewish-American Imagination* (Bloomington: Indiana University Press, 1987); and Alan M. Wald, *The New York Intellectuals: The Rise and Decline of the Anti-Stalinist Left From the 1930s to the 1980s* (Chapel Hill: University of North Carolina Press, 1987). On the Jewishness of the New York Intellectuals, see Ruth R. Wisse, "The New York (Jewish) Intellectuals," *Commentary* 84 (November 1987): 28–38; and Edward S. Shapiro, "Jewishness and the New York Intellectual," *Judaism* 38 (1989): 282–92. On a counter-tradition of Jewish intellectuals, see: Carole S. Kessner, ed., *The "Other" New York Jewish Intellectuals* (New York: New York University Press, 1994).

42   Howe, "The Lost Young Intellectual," 152, 163, 153, 163. Howe's article appeared originally in *Commentary* 2 (1946). See Donald Weber's insightful reading of Howe's essay below. On the creation of the myth of the rootless Jewish intellectual, particularly in relation to Bellow, see Mark Shechner, "Saul Bellow and Ghetto Cosmopolitanism," in *The Conversion of the Jews and Other Essays* (London:

Macmillan, 1990), pp. 31–42. The essay appears as well in Vinoda and Shiv Kumar, eds., *Saul Bellow: A Symposium on the Jewish Heritage*, pp. 125–36.

43 For Bellow, the characteristic defining element of Jewish literature is, indeed, an element of style, its "curious" mingling of "laughter and trembling." See his introduction to *Great Jewish Short Stories*, p. 12.

44 Hannah Arendt, "The Jew as Pariah: A Hidden Tradition," in Arthur A. Cohen, ed., *Arguments and Doctrines: A Reader in Jewish Thinking After the Holocaust* (Philadelphia: The Jewish Publication Society and Harper & Row, 1970), pp. 27, 28. The essay was originally published in *The Reconstructionist* 25 (March 20, 1959): 3–9 and (April 3, 1959): 8–14.

45 Daniel Bell, "A Parable of Alienation," in Harold Ribalow, *Mid-century: An Anthology of Jewish Life and Culture in Our Times*, p. 143. Bell's article was originally published in *Jewish Frontier* (November 1946): 12–19.

46 Isaac Deutscher, "The Non-Jewish Jew," in *The Non-Jewish Jew and Other Essays* (Boston: Alyson Publications, 1982), pp. 25–6. The essay was originally delivered as a lecture in 1958. On Elisha ben Avuya, see Babylonian Talmud, Tractate Hagiga 14b ff. It is interesting that Deutscher transliterates his name incorrectly (perhaps a matter of dialect) and mistranslates "Akher" as "the stranger," an attempt (perhaps) at inserting the theme of alienation. "Non-Jewish Jew" was a term of opprobrium in use before Deutscher began to use it honorifically.

47 Arendt, "The Jew as Pariah," p. 28.

48 Bell, "A Parable of Alienation," p. 137.

49 Alfred Kazin, "The Jew as Modern Writer," *Commentary* (April 1966): 39. This essay also appears as the introduction to Norman Podhoretz, ed., *The Commentary Reader: Two Decades of Articles and Stories* (New York: Atheneum, 1966).

50 I have compiled this list from the various articles discussed in this section.

51 Deutscher, "The Non-Jewish Jew," pp. 27, 26, 27.

52 Kazin, "The Jew as Modern Writer," 39.

53 Arendt, "The Jew as Pariah," p. 27.

54 Ruth R. Wisse, "The New York (Jewish) Intellectuals," 28.

55 Martin Greenberg, "Modern Man as Jew," *Commentary* 5 (1948): 86. The article is a review of Bellow's *The Victim*.

56 Bell, "Parable of Alienation," pp. 133, 134.

57 Harold Fisch, *The Dual Image: A Study of the Jew in English Literature* (London: World Jewish Library, 1971), p. 116.

58 Fiedler, "Saul Bellow," p. 58.

59 Kazin, "The Jew as Modern Writer," 41.

60 Bernard Malamud, "Jewishness in American Fiction," in *Talking Horse: Bernard Malamud on Life and Work*, ed., Alan Chase and Nicholas Delbanco (New York: Columbia University Press, 1996), p. 137.

61 Fiedler, "Saul Bellow," p. 64; Fiedler, "The Jew in the American Novel," in *To the Gentiles*, p. 115; Fiedler, "Saul Bellow," p. 64.

62 Bellow, Introduction to *Great Jewish Short Stories*, p. 14.

63 On descent as a crucial element in the construction of ethnic identity, see Werner Sollors, *Beyond Ethnicity: Consent and Descent in American Culture* (New York: Oxford University Press, 1986). On the resilience and significance of the concept of race in writing about ethnic culture, see Anthony Appiah, "The Uncompleted Argument: Du Bois and the Illusion of Race," in Henry Louis Gates, Jr. ed., *"Race," Writing, and Difference* (Chicago: University of Chicago Press, 1986), pp. 21–37; and Walter Benn Michaels, "Race into Culture: A Critical Genealogy of Cultural Identity," *Critical Inquiry* 18 (1992): 654–85. On the centrality of "race" in Jewish thought, see: Daniel Boyarin and Jonathan Boyarin, "Diaspora: Generation and the Ground of Jewish Identity," *Critical Inquiry* 19 (1993): 693–725. See also Daniel Boyarin, *Carnal Israel: Reading Sex in Talmudic Culture* (Berkeley: University of California Press, 1993), pp. 1–30. My own, "Race, Literary History, and the 'Jewish' Question," is forthcoming.

2

"Who's he when he's at home?":
Saul Bellow's Translations

HANA WIRTH-NESHER

A S A CHILD of Jewish immigrants in Montreal, Saul Bellow
did not know English as his mother tongue. Yiddish was
the language of home, Hebrew of the synagogue and religious
school. So as Bellow acquired English – indeed, embraced it and
enriched it with his writing – he did so within hearing range of
both Yiddish and Hebrew. Writers who emerge out of these mul-
tilingual circumstances are always, in effect, translators. Thus any
discussion of Bellow's Jewishness must contend with the linguistic and intertextual: In what ways and to what extent do other
languages and texts shape Bellow's writing? To answer this question, I want first to relate three separate acts of translation in
three distinct fictive spaces, and then to examine the dynamic
among them, a dynamic that takes place in an imaginary cultural
space. The translations were all performed by Bellow within one
decade, 1953–1963.

Translation #1. Three years before the publication of *Seize the
Day*, Saul Bellow translated and published a story by Isaac Bashevis Singer that became a milestone in the Jewish-American literary landscape. With the appearance of "Gimpel the Fool" in
English in *Partisan Review* in 1953, Singer was launched as the
poet laureate of the American Jewish community; the world that
he invented in his fictions, where the boundaries between the

I am indebted to the Longfellow Institute at Harvard University for providing a stimulating forum to test these ideas. My thanks also to Sacvan
Bercovitch, Zephyra Porat, Marc Shell, Werner Sollors, and Ruth Wisse for
helpful comments, to Malki Keisy and Amit Yahav for research assistance,
and to the Israel Science Foundation for generous support.

25

natural and supernatural are indistinguishable, became the lost Old World to which American Jews have made both imaginary and, more recently, literal pilgrimages. But there was "as much cover-up as exposure in Bellow's 'Gimpel,' " for the Americanization of the story in the translation contributed to a collective cultural amnesia.[1]

In the Yiddish story, "Gimpel Tam," an outcast in his village is repeatedly tricked, fooled, and ridiculed by his neighbors, a fate to which he is resigned. The rational, empirical world has no hold on Gimpel whose gullibility makes him a saintly fool, and whose love for his children overrides his pride at being the town's much taunted failure. As the Hebrew word "tam" means "innocent, "honest," "pure," or "simpleton" as well as "fool," his very name opens up a gap in the text that has captivated readers for decades. Finally, Gimpel's wife's deathbed confession that she has deceived him all along and that his children are not his drives him to the devil who incites him to do evil. In a godless universe which is only a "thick mire," Satan urges him to take revenge on the town by defiling the loaves of bread in the bakery so that his deceivers eat filth. Gimpel has every reason to distrust but chooses to trust nevertheless, for "the longer I lived the more I understood that there were really no lies. . . . Whatever doesn't really happen is dreamed at night. Often I heard tales of which I said, 'Now this is a thing that cannot happen.' But before a year had elapsed I heard that it actually had come to pass somewhere."[2]

In translating for a *Partisan Review* readership removed from Judaic texts and sources a story originally intended for an audience well versed in Jewish tradition, Bellow retained only seven Yiddish words: *golem, mezzuzah, chalah, kreplach, schnorrer, dybbuk,* and *Tisha B'av*. With the exception of the last term, an annual day of mourning and fasting to commemorate the destruction of the Second Temple and the resulting two millennia of exile, these terms had already seeped into the American Jewish lexicon, in part through familiarity with literary works about dybbuks and golems[3] and in part through popular culture, culinary and other. Retaining words such as *chalah* underscored the quaint ethnic character of the story while also providing a few "authentic" markers of the lost culture. Actual liturgical references, however, no matter how common, were converted into American equivalents. And this is where the cross-cultural plot thickens. For in the English translation of "Gimpel," Bellow translated the well-known Hebrew prayer for the dead, "El molei rachamim" into the Christian "God 'a mercy," a shift that transformed Gimpel's Eastern European setting into Southern Baptist terrain.[4]

Translation #2. In Bellow's novella *Seize the Day*, published only three years later (also in *Partisan Review*) there is only one non-English rupture into the text. When Tommy Wilhelm remembers a visit to his mother's graveside, he recalls the *same* Hebrew prayer for the dead passed over in "Gimpel." Here is the passage, in which Bellow translates the Hebrew for his English-speaking readers:

At the cemetery Wilhelm had paid a man to say a prayer for her. He was among the tombs and he wanted to be tipped for the *El molei rachamin.* "Thou God of Mercy," Wilhelm thought that meant. *B'gan Aden* – "in Paradise." Singing, they drew it out. *B'gan Ay-den.*

In other words, what was erased in the English translation of the Yiddish story reappears, what was repressed comes back to haunt the pages of Bellow's American story set in New York, the story of another man who is a failure in his community, who is gullible, tricked, and repeatedly deceived. This is not simply a matter of influence, of Singer's story bearing down upon Bellow's; it is an intertextual referent that places Bellow's work in relation to both Hebrew and Yiddish as purveyors of a lost civilization, the Jewish world annihilated in the Holocaust. It is apt that the only non-English in Bellow's text is a prayer for the dead.

Translation #3. Less than six years after the publication of *Seize the Day*, Bellow edited a collection of Jewish fiction entitled *Great Jewish Short Stories*. Bellow selected and arranged the pieces, wrote headings for each one in order to introduce these writers to his American public, and included an introduction in which he defines the essence of Jewish storytelling. Jewish literature, he wrote, is marked by an ambivalent stance toward life in which "laughter and trembling are so curiously mingled that it is not easy to determine the relations of the two."[5] The introduction makes clear that Bellow is captivated by writers who lived between languages and often chose to write in languages other than the one that enveloped them as children: Joseph Conrad the Pole who "loved England and the English language" or Isaac Babel, "put in charge of publishing the works of Sholem Aleichem in Yiddish" and yet who wrote in Russian, in the language of the perpetrators of the pogrom to which he was witness. "Who was Babel? Where did he come from?" asks Bellow.

Twenty authors are represented in the collection, along with one excerpt from the Bible, and nine of the writers are identified with Yiddish language and culture, either as writers, translators, or editors. One strategy for making these authors accessible and attractive was to "translate" their contributions into Anglo-American equivalents. As chronology is the main structuring principle of the volume, his first selection is, predictably, from the Bible, but a rather idiosyncratic choice: the apocryphal Book of Tobit which Bellow describes as a story about a man "in exile [who] cannot forget that he is a Jew." To make Tobit's story comprehensible to his readers, Bellow goes on to say "It is possible to compare him with Joyce's Leopold Bloom."[6] Thus the first work of Jewish literature in the collection is Jewish because the character conforms to a *fin de siècle* typology of Jewishness as constructed by a high modernist Irish writer in an English novel. Bellow is undoubtedly right in assuming that more of his readers would have heard of Leopold Bloom than of Tobit, and those who knew of Bloom most surely regarded him as the archetypal Jew. In addition to the many ironies inherent in such a presentation of Jewish literature is the fact that Bloom, from any Jewish legal perspective, isn't a Jew at all (something Joyce certainly knew) but is very much the construction of Jewishness prevalent in turn-of-the-century European civilization.[7]

Thus, the translations. In each case, Bellow positions himself as a cultural mediator, the man who translates from one culture to another. Taken together, they testify to the echo of another language and another culture in Bellow's consciousness and writing. What are the cultural implications of each of these acts of translation within and between the texts?

In the case of Bellow's translation of "Gimpel," not only did he transform Hebrew liturgy as it is embedded in Yiddish civilization into Christian parlance, he also omitted any phrase that in Singer's original either parodied Judaism or, more to the point, ridiculed Christianity. The village rowdies taunt Gimpel with crude verses such as "El Melekh – katchke drei dikh" (roughly "Our Lord in Heaven, the hen laid seven"), a blasphemous parody of liturgy which does not appear in the English translation. And in defense of his gullibility in the face of persistent mockery from the townspeople, particularly when he refuses to doubt his paternity of the child born to Elka only seventeen weeks after their as yet unconsummated marriage, Gimpel appeals to the mass gullibility of Christians, "ver veyst? ot zogt men dokh as s'yoyzl hot in gantsn keyn tatn nisht gehat" ("Who knows? They say that Jesus didn't have any father at all"). This somewhat coarse and demeaning reference to Jesus (the diminutive "yoyzl") could be offensive to Christians, and although, according to Bellow, it was the volume's editor Eliezer Greenberg who deleted it when he dictated the story to Bellow, neither Singer nor Bellow had it reinstated in subsequent printings of the English text. Anti-ecumenical, maybe, in 1953, the decade of the timid emergence of Jewish-American literature in the shadow of the Holocaust. In any event, it was a risk that neither Singer nor Greenberg, nor subsequently Bellow, wanted to take.[8]

And now what about *Seize the Day*, the most anthologized and discussed of Bellow's work? In that novella, what exactly has Tommy, the central protagonist, "forgotten"? What has Bellow "forgotten"? And what do we need to "remember" in order to read this text? One way to approach these questions is to examine the names. Formerly Wilhelm Adler, Bellow's main character changed his name to Tommy Wilhelm in order to invent an American self destined for what he hoped would be a Hollywood success story. In changing his name, Tommy has damaged his patrilineage, severing himself from a father portrayed throughout the novella as repeatedly rejecting his son for failing to live up to his expectations. "He had cast off his father's name, and with it his father's opinion of him" (25). Tommy is a far more American name than Wilhelm, one that trails behind it any number of American heroes, from Thomas Jefferson and Tom Paine to Tom Sawyer and Tom and Jerry. The Americanizing of the name is also a Christianizing, for Thomas is one of the twelve disciples, ironically the one who did not believe in the resurrection without empirical proof, ''doubting Thomas.'' The name ''Tommy'' or ''Tom'' is obviously a homonym for ''Gimpel Tam'' (pronounced ''tom''), the gullible but saintly fool of Singer's story. Tommy Wilhelm, then, is situated between the Yiddish Gimpel Tam and the Christian-American Tom.

The word ''tom'' functions in *Seize the Day* as a syllepsis in the sense that Michael Riffaterre has recently used this term in his discussion of intertexuality:

a word that has two mutually incompatible meanings, one acceptable in the context in which the word appears, the other valid only in the intertext to which the word also belongs and that it represents at the surface of the text, as the tip of an iceberg. The syllepsis' power over the reader lies in the paradoxical combination of two factors. One is the unmistakable obviousness of the connective, the other is the distance between the connected texts.[9]

In Bellow's case, what his translation repressed, namely the specifically Jewish liturgical reference, ''El molei rachamim,'' reappears in his subsequent fictional world. But the choice of his protagonist's name, Tom, evokes and represses all of Singer's story and world. ''It takes a whole text to compensate for the disappearance of the repressed intertext,'' continues Riffaterre, in what serves as an apt description of what transpires between Bellow and Singer. ''Thus, the intertext is to the text what the unconcious is to consciousness.''[10]

Bellow's relation to Singer exemplifies a defining feature of Jewish-American literature. For Bellow, Singer serves as a point of departure, an origin, an authentic past that has been annihilated, lost through tragic history and also abandoned in the will to assimilate; Singer can be evoked for the sake of some continuity with a collective identity other than Christian America. That it should be Singer is particularly charged, for the signature of his work is its repudiation of the rational satiric Yiddish literary tradition that preceded him and its construction of a pre-modern

Yiddish folk culture pervaded by the supernatural and the work-
ings of the devil.[11] As a post-Holocaust Yiddish writer, Singer
reinstates evil and the irrational to this predominantly rationalist
tradition with a vengeance. Bellow, the liberal humanist writer
who has repeatedly denounced modernist artists for being purveyors of nihilism and who has affirmed man's potential for
goodness, also has never lost sight of the powers of darkness. As
he too writes in the shadow of the Holocaust, Bellow in the
1950s walks a tightrope between two collective identities prevalent throughout the two decades following the war: the self-
reliant American Adam and his liberal humanist offspring and
the saintly Jewish victim, witness to humanity's capacity for evil.

   Renate Lachmann, in her study on text and memory, has recently suggested that "The space between texts and the space
within texts that develops in the experience of intertextual space,
produce a tension . . . that must be endured by the reader. The
space of memory is inscribed in a text in the same way that a
text inscribes itself in a memory space. The memory of a text is
its intertextuality."[12] If "intertextuality demonstrates the process
by which a culture continually rewrites and retranscribes itself,"
then the Singer-Bellow intertextual dynamic can be instructive
regarding the rewriting of Jewish literary memory. Singer's Yiddish text, composed and read in a diglossic environment, inscribes Hebrew prayers such as "El molei rachamim" without
translating them, as his readers are conversant with Jewish liturgy and hence can shift easily to and from the Hebrew references. These are not ruptures in the text; they are seamless tran-
sitions. As the audience for the *translated* Singer is neither
bilingual nor diglossic, the linguistic shift from Hebrew to Yiddish, from the sacred to the profane, is not retained but flattened
into one language, and even that is translated into an American
religious equivalent (note the dialect – "God 'a mercy" – to mark
the discourse of folk prayer and regional customs). But since the
cultural agenda for translating Singer is to carve out a place for
him in both modernist *Partisan Review* circles and a tradition of
Yiddish literature that is continuous with Jewish civilization,
some Yiddish must be retained to provide the ethnic and "authenticating" flavor, which accounts for the culinary and folklor-

istic terms that the secular American reader would be more likely to recognize. In the third translation, from "Gimpel" into the American novella *Seize the Day*, the Yiddish all but disappears (with the exception of the homonym "tam," derived from the Hebraic repertoire of the Yiddish language), and the religious phrase "El molei rachamim" is reinstated (with a much more dignified translation, "Thou God of Mercy") as Jewish civilization loses its bilingual dimension and is transformed in America into Judaism, the third great religion. Bellow's text "remembers" the prayer, but in an entirely different context. It remembers what it needs in its new cultural landscape.

Several of the other names in the text contribute to this dynamic between languages and cultures. Bearing a German-Jewish name, Dr. Adler takes pride in his rational and calculated approach to life, and is depicted as a preening elderly gentleman with fastidious Old World manners. His name, meaning eagle in German, also conveys this air of nobility. It is the German Jew Dr. Adler who gave his son the overbearing and obtrusive name of a Prussian emperor. In his kindly patronizing moments, he Anglicizes it to "Wilky." As Adler is the name that gives away Tommy's Jewishness, he prefers to discard it and to retain the Germanic Wilhelm, a sardonic twist in the early 1950s, less than ten years from the Holocaust. Tommy is painfully aware of and embarrassed by his father's theatricality, his studied patrician manner. As translator of Yiddish literature and conversant with modern Yiddish culture, Bellow conferred on Tommy's father the same name as the acclaimed Yiddish stage actor, Jacob P. Adler. The most talked about Yiddish performer of the first third of the century, Jacob Adler cultivated a style of "high bravura" in and out of the theater. As Irving Howe put it, "by sheer force of will and blessing of physique, [he] intended to prove that a Jew could make himself into an aristocrat."[13] His first important role was in Jacob Gordin's *Jewish King Lear*, prototype of dramas about the narcissistic father who rejects his child. Adler's name compounds the ironies in this novella in that the son's miserable failure as an actor in Hollywood is contrasted with the bravura of his theatrical father, whose name links him with the most successful of actors – on the Yiddish stage.

The substitute father for Tommy in *Seize the Day* is the trickster Dr. Tamkin, whose name suggests his affinity with Wilhelm. Both Tommy and Tamkin are diminutives of Tom, the former in English and the latter in Middle German (and consequently in Yiddish). When Tamkin presents to Tommy his theory about the coexistence of two souls in each person, the real and the pretender souls, Wilhelm reflects that "in Tommy he saw the pretender. And even Wilky might not be himself. Might the name of the true soul be the one by which his old grandfather had called him – Velvel?" Here Wilhelm appeals to Jewish tradition as an authenticating source, nostalgically suggesting that his Yiddish name is his real identity. But although he wistfully entertains the idea that his genuine self may lie in his Yiddish name, his conclusion is universal, "The name of a soul, however, must be only that – soul. What did it look like? Does my soul look like me?" (72).

Tommy Wilhelm has two fathers in this book, each representative of a stereotype from recent Jewish history: the rational but stuffy German Jew (Adler) and the superstitious but ardent and impetuous Eastern European Jew (Tamkin). But like Jay Gatz, he changes his name to give birth to a romantic image of himself, to become the self-made American individualist. "The changed name was a mistake, and he would admit it as freely as you liked. But this mistake couldn't be undone now, so why must his father continually remind him how he had sinned?" (25). Just as the son has rejected the father, so too has the father rejected his son, doing so in Christian terms: " 'You want to make yourself into my cross. I'll see you dead, Wilky, by Christ, before I let you do that to me" (110).

The assimilated German-Jewish father abandons his son in order not to be cast in the role of Christ, after having warned Tommy previously, "I want nobody on my back. Get off! And I give you the same advice, Wilky. Carry nobody on your back!"(55). Abandoned by his biological father, Tommy fantasizes a better father for himself who *will* carry him on his back, "And Wilhelm realized that he was on Tamkin's back. It made him feel that he had virtually left the ground and was riding upon the other man. He was in the air. It was for Tamkin to take the steps'' (96). Eventually abandoned by Tamkin as well, Tommy reproaches himself for self-delusion: ''I was the man beneath; Tamkin was on my back, and I thought I was on his'' (105). Far from the image which this recalls, Aeneas leaving behind a burning and ruined civilization with his aged father Anchises on his back, Tommy is left alone at the story's end with no fathers to comfort him as he grieves over the body of a stranger who has come to represent himself.

Whereas Gimpel the Fool in his traditional religious community is deceived by the sexton's wife, the matchmaker, the rabbi's daughter, and by nearly everyone in the town, Tommy is deceived in the two main arenas where he most aspires to success: by the theater agent, Maurice Venice, and by the stock market agent, Dr. Tamkin. Maurice Venice is the director of a company named Kaskasia Productions, a play on the Hebrew words ''kas-kas'' or ''kash-kash'' either of which casts ridicule on the character. The former translates into scales (as on fish) or dandruff, and the latter refers to babble or sheer nonsense. Hollywood, the American dream machine invented in part by Jewish immigrants, seems flaky, fishy (''Was there perhaps something fishy about this Maurice Venice?'' [18]), and nonsensical, puns which are available to the reader familiar with the other languages lurking in the text and which constitute another tantalizing case of cultural syllepsis.

Nor do the Jewish intertextual references stop here. As has already been recognized in previous interpretations of *Seize the Day*, Bellow alludes to the vehement antagonism in nineteenth century Jewish history between Hasidim and their opponents, the maskilim, adherents of the Enlightenment. The most conspicuous evidence lies in the surnames of two key minor figures, Mr. Perls and Mr. Rappaport. Joseph Perl was the author of a scathing satire of Hasidism entitled *Revealer of Secrets*, whose main character bears a striking resemblance to Tamkin, the modern conjuror and trickster in *Seize the Day*. His contemporary Judah Leib Rappaport, was an Austrian rabbi and the author of many scholarly articles and criticisms regarding Hasidism. ''The fictional Perls and Rappaport function as secular *maskilim*, frequently passing judgement on Tamkin and Wilhelm.''[14] In Wilhelm's intensely emotional rather than rational attitude toward life, it is possible to see a modern Jewish-American analogue of the Hasid, particularly in his romantic love of his fellow man, ''a general love for all these imperfect and lurid-looking people burst out in Wilhelm's breast. He loved them. One and all, he passionately loved them'' (84). It is also very Whitmanesque. ''And the great, great crowd, the inexhaustible current of millions of every race and kind pouring out, pressing round, of every age, of every genius, possessors of every human secret, antique and future, in every face the refinement of one particular motive or essence'' (115).

The coexistence of two cultures and two textual repertoires characterizes *Seize the Day*. The novella repeatedly invokes a double inheritance as perceived by Jewish-Americans of Bellow's generation. He navigates between two worlds, two discourses, and two audiences. The very title of the work alludes to the *carpe diem* philosophy as it is expressed in English poetry and in American literature and ideology: a surrender to the present, a sanctification of the moment, a forgetting. *Seize the Day* is motivated, however, by Tommy Wilhelm's inability to act on this advice, his incessant involuntary remembering. The imperative to remember that characterizes Jewish culture surfaces in the words of the Hebrew prayer, in Rappaport's reminder to Tommy to attend memorial prayers on Yom Kippur (''Yizkor''), the very antithesis of *carpe diem*. The words of advice to ''seize the day'' are uttered by Tamkin, the impetuous, trickster figure who on the one hand persuades him to invest in lard (no doubt why he squirms when confronted with the graffiti, ''Do Not Sin'' and ''Do Not Eat the Pig'') and on the other hand suggests that Tommy's ''real'' name is the Yiddish one given him by his grandfather. To place the *carpe diem* bidding and the American behest not to dwell on the past in the mouth of the character most clumsy with English words (his poem is execrable) and most associated with Wilhelm's Jewish roots is to cast suspicion on the ''seize the day'' philosophy altogether. The opposition of the title and the text reenacts the cultural oppositions throughout the work.

Bellow evokes the English literary tradition through three intertexts: Shakespeare's sonnet on love in the face of death ("love that well which thou must leave ere long"); Milton's elegy *Lycidas* ("sunk though he be beneath the wat'ry floor"); Keats's romantic lament *Endymion* (Come then, sorrow! I thought to leave thee/and deceive thee,/But now of all the world I love thee best"). The poems by Shakespeare and Keats stress the intensity of the present; Milton's elegy, in contrast, is the keen, deliberate remembering in the act of mourning. Bellow inscribes fragments of these prominent poems of the English tradition into a contrastive environment of public spaces in New York of the 1950s: hotels, stock brokers' offices, cafeterias, sidewalks and intersections, public baths, and funeral parlors. To the extent that the stock market, movies, and baseball – all games of one sort or another that require immersion in the present – propel this world, it is markedly American. But it is also peopled by characters who evince another world, European and Jewish, that underscore history and remembrance.

Bellow's ambivalence about the Jewish motifs in his work is evident in his revision of *Seize the Day*. In the first version published in *Partisan Review* (as Michael Kramer notes in his introduction to this volume) Tommy finds himself in a funeral home that is unambiguously Jewish: "The white of the stained glass window was like mother-of-pearl, the blue of the Star of David like velvet ribbon."[15] But for publication in book form, Bellow revised the ending so that the religious identity of the funeral home is left for the reader to intuit, "The white of the stained glass was like mother-of-pearl, with the blue of a great star fluid, like velvet ribbon" (116). In this revised version, Tommy moves further away from Jewish identification and closer to Christian America. "Oh, Father, what do I ask of you?" suggests that he is a Christ figure, as does the reference to his children. "What'll I do about the kids – Tommy, Paul?" As if the names Thomas and Paul were not enough, the Christianizing is compounded by the violation of European Jewish practice in naming a son for a living father. There appears to be no moving toward neutral ground; there is only movement toward Gentile America. Whereas in the earlier version Tommy "found the secret consummation of his heart's ultimate need," in the final version he sank "*toward* [my italics] the consummation of his heart's ultimate need," with the emphasis on movement, not stasis.

The question of what is "forgotten" and what is "remembered" can be examined within various forms of intertextuality: participation, troping, and transformation. Participation is the dialogical sharing in texts of a written culture. This would clearly be the case in Singer's quotation from the prayer book, for this is repetition for the sake of continuity in a given culture. It is the pleasure and assurance of repetition. Troping, on the other hand, is a turning away from the precursor text; "it is an attempt to surpass, defend against and eradicate traces of a precursor's text." All of the de-Judaizing instances, the omissions of potentially offensive passages for an implied non-Jewish reader, would be instances of troping, whether it be the Greenberg-Bellow-Singer collaborative deletion of whole sentences or Bellow's excision of the Star of David in his revision of *Seize the Day* for book publication. Finally, transformation involves the appropriation of other texts through a process of distancing them; "it conceals the other texts, veils them, plays with them, renders them unrecognizable."[16] This is where I would place the syllepsis, the homonym "tam" which rewrites the Hebraic/Yiddish story into the American story. The transformative establishes a third imaginary space; in the case of Bellow's novella *Seize the Day*, it invents one model of Jewish-American literature. The imaginary space that this new literature occupies can be expressed only through fictive texts, which in turn are necessarily intertextual, and in the case of Jewish literature, often interlinguistic as well. The translations that occur in this type of ethnic literature do not simply negotiate between cultures but rather, as Walter Benjamin has put it, they make "both the original and the translation recognizable as fragments of a greater language, just as fragments are part of a vessel."[17]

By translating Singer's "Gimpel" into American English, Bellow has crossed the boundary to the past, but he has reshaped the representation of that past so that it achieves both continuity and discontinuity, both survival of the Yiddish text for Jewish literature and accommodation of that text to American literature for American readers. By inscribing Hebrew into the English text of *Seize the Day*, Bellow steers his American readers into an encounter with an "other" language and culture, but he also translates that Hebrew into its American Judaic equivalent, into the terms of the religious pluralism of America of the 1950s.[18] By translating Tobit into Bloom, Bellow "remembers" one textual tradition by crossing over into an "other" textual repertoire. The guiding principle in this mapping of Jewish literature for Bellow is linguistic and cultural hybridity.

Finally, what do all of these interlinguistic and intercultural references amount to? Certainly they are evidence that we are dealing with a writer one generation removed from immigration who navigates between two languages and traditions and who takes on the role of cultural mediator for more than one readership. He is the one who introduces non-Jewish readers to Jewish literature that has been "translated" into the terms of Anglo-American modernism and rendered nonthreatening to the Christian Other. Yet in another sense, he is the purveyor of Jewish texts for a Jewish English-speaking audience that may be knowledgeable enough about Jewish history to comprehend the specific Jewish references mentioned previously, but may also be anxious to see that literature as compatible with prevailing ideologies and poetics. This would make Bellow a classic example of the author of ethnic literature, which has been traditionally defined as a literature of "otherness" in opposition to a more central or mainstream literature. Yet such a definition presupposes stable, consistent, and essential definitions of two cultures that are in opposition to each other. I would prefer to regard ethnic literature in Werner Sollors' terms as "an interplay of different ancestries." It is the third imaginary place that is provided by the fictionalizing act.[19]

This brings me back to my third case of translation: Bellow's equivalence of the Book of Tobit and Joyce's *Ulysses* in his preface to the first selection in *Great Jewish Short Stories*. Tobit is an apocryphal book, the story of a Hebrew exile in Assyria who endangered his life by defying a royal decree in order to bury his people's dead. Scholars are still disputing whether the original language was Hebrew or Aramaic (fragments of the book were found among the scrolls at Qumran in both languages), but the only full text is the Greek. Tobit was a book congenial to early Christian Reformers, notably Luther who suggested it as a subject for comedy. The character of Leopold Bloom is a "translation" or transformation of the "original" Greek Odysseus into the son of a convert to Christianity, who is identified by his fellow Irishmen as a Jew. "Who's he when he's at home?" asks Molly Bloom, when she runs across the word "metempsychosis" in the Calypso chapter of the novel. True to his function as the Irish/Jewish/ Christian reincarnation of Ulysses, Bloom turns translator for Molly: "transmigration of souls," he explains. Just as Joyce's novel reenacts this transmigration of souls through a poetics of translation across civilizations, so Bellow's *Seize the Day* is part of an intertextual and intercultural enactment of translations located in the space of Jewish-American literature. In the spirit of Molly's question, then, we may ask – who's Bellow when *he's* at home?

NOTES

1 Sidra De Koven Ezrahi, "State and Real Estate: Territoriality and the Modern Jewish Imagination," in *Terms of Survival: The Jewish World since 1945* (London: Routledge, 1995), p. 50.
2 Isaac Bashevis Singer, "Gimpel Tam," *A Treasury of Yiddish Stories*, eds. Irving Howe and Eliezer Greenberg (New York: Viking Press, 1953), p. 413.
3 Some of these Yiddish words are included in English dictionaries such as *The American Heritage College Dictionary* which defines a *dybbuk* as "the wandering soul of a dead person that enters the body of a living person and controls his or her behavior" (428) and *golem* as "an artificially created human being supernaturally endowed with life" (584). Bellow's Jewish readers with some familiarity of Yiddish culture would have known S. Ansky's famous play *The Dybbuk* as well as many versions of the Golem story such as Gustav Meyrink's book published in 1928.
4 Sidra Ezrahi was the first to point this out: "The distance between 'God 'a mercy' and 'El Maleh rahamim' is, it seems, the terrain that

Gimpel *tam* must cross in order to enter the pages of *Partisan Review* and become naturalized on American soil." "State and Real Estate," p. 51.

5 Saul Bellow, ed., *Great Jewish Short Stories* (New York: Dell Publishing Company, 1963), p. 12.

6 Bellow, ed., *Great Jewish Short Stories*, p. 17.

7 For discussions of such constructions of Jewishness see Bryan Cheyette, *Constructions of 'the Jew' in English Literature and Society* (New York: Cambridge University Press, 1993); Sander Gilman, *The Jew's Body* (London: Routledge, 1991); and Linda Nochlin and Tamar Garb, eds., *The Jew in the Text* (London: Thames and Hudson, 1996).

8 According to Howe

I inveigled Saul Bellow, not quite so famous yet, to do the translation. Bellow had a pretty good command of Yiddish, but not quite enough to do the story on his own. So we sat down before a typewriter in Lazer's [Eliezer Greenberg] apartment on East Nineteenth Street, Lazer read out the Yiddish sentence by sentence, Saul occasionally asked about refinements of meaning, and I watched in a state of high enchantment. Three or four hours, and it was done. Saul took another half hour to go over the translation and then, excited, read aloud the version that has since become famous. It was a feat of virtuosity, and we drank a schnapps to celebrate. (Irving Howe, *A Margin of Hope: An Intellectual Autobiography* [New York: Harcourt Brace Jovanovich, 1982], p. 262.)

I am grateful to Ruth Wisse for bringing this to my attention and for sharing with me her unpublished manuscript, "The Repression of Aggression: Translation of Yiddish into English." Bellow's translation of "Gimpel the Fool" has been reprinted in many collections, among them volumes edited by Howe, Bellow, and Singer. Irving Howe, *Jewish-American Stories* (New York: New American Library, 1977); Bellow's collection mentioned above; Isaac Bashevis Singer, *The Collected Stories* (New York: Farrar, Straus & Giroux,1982).

9 Michael Riffaterre, "Compulsory Reader Response: the Intertextual Drive," in *Intertextuality: Theories and Practices*, eds. Michael Worton and Judith Still (Manchester: Manchester University Press, 1990), p. 71.

10 Riffaterre, "Compulsory Reader Response: the Intertextual Drive," p. 77.

11 See David G. Roskies, *A Bridge of Longing: the Lost Art of Yiddish Storytelling* (Cambridge, Mass.: Harvard University Press, 1995), pp. 266–307.

12 Renate Lachmann, *Memory and Literature: Intertextuality in Russian Modernism* (Minneapolis: University of Minnesota, 1997), p. 15.

13 Irving Howe, *World of Our Fathers* (New York: Simon and Schuster, 1976), p. 473.

14 S. Lillian Kremer, "*Seize the Day*: Intimations of Anti-Hasidic Satire," *Modern Jewish Studies Annual* and *Yiddish* 4 (1982): 37.

15 Bellow, "Seize the Day," *Partisan Review* 23:3 (1956), p. 431.

16 Lachmann, *Memory and Literature*, pp. 17–19.

17 Walter Benjamin, "The Task of the Translator," *Illuminations* (New York: Schocken, 1969), p. 78.

18 Translatability, according to Iser, entails "two important spheres of human life, memory and otherness, both of which are marked by a boundary-crossing. . . . Memory crosses boundaries to a past; otherness crosses boundaries to an outside." In Wolfgang Iser, "Coda to the Discussion," in *The Translatability of Culture: Figurations of the Space Between*, eds. Sanford Budick and Wolfgang Iser (Stanford: Stanford University Press, 1996), p. 297.

19 Werner Sollors, "Literature and Ethnicity," *Harvard Encyclopedia of American Ethnic Groups*, ed. Stephen Thernstrom (Cambridge, Mass.: Harvard University Press, 1980), p. 648.

3

Manners and Morals, Civility and Barbarism: The Cultural Contexts of *Seize the Day*

DONALD WEBER

The next conduct will have to come from the heart, from attach-
ment to life despite the worst it has shown us, and it has shown us
just about everything.
  – Saul Bellow, "The Trip to Galena" (1950)[1]

I have known Bellow for more than half a century . . . and feel I
understand the springs of his talent – which have to do with his
innate sense of the primitive sources of life.
  – Alfred Kazin (1996)[2]

ROM CIVILITY I now have some pain in my belly,' " laments Moses Herzog, trying on pants.[3] Saul Bellow's comic
intellectual-schlemiel-hero, the voluble talker from the prize-
winning novel *Herzog* (1964), voices perhaps *the* cosmic
complaint that, for over fifty years, has occupied Bellow's various
literary alter egos. What does it mean for Herzog to speak of a
"pain from civility"? Why should "civility" induce such discom-
fort in everyday life? For Bellow, at least, the answers are complex, for the costs of "achieving" civilized behavior – as expressed by manners, "higher" education, belief systems (as
proposed by theoreticians of various orientation, spiritual and
political), and tempered, psychological "adjustment" to the over-
whelming "distractedness" (another of Bellow's key words) of
our world – are measured in affective repression and denial. Civility masks and obscures what Bellow often terms our individual
"souls," or "essence" – "the characteristic signature of a person."
Civility inhibits and thwarts our necessary quest for "un-
earth[ing] buried essences" that the clutter and growth of the
modern world shroud, often in the name of material and tech-
nological progress.[4] Above all, civility pains because as we em-

43

brace – or conform to – its exacting demands, or strive to attain its surface appearance, we unwittingly labor against what, at the very end of *Seize the Day* (1956), Bellow famously calls "the consummation of [our] heart's ultimate need" (118): the need to connect, at the level of raw, unmediated *feelings*, with the deeper currents of our being, the enabling consciousness of our "essence" as feeling human beings linked to others through bonds of human solidarity and identification.

I realize that all this high-level abstraction with respect to Bellow's fundamental themes may seem a bit pretentious, perhaps even downright obscure to the first-time reader of *Seize the Day*. After all, what does all this talk of "essences" and "distraction," of civility and manners have to do with the narrative of that sad sack Tommy Wilhelm, his stern, aloof father, and the bizarre philosopher-speculator Dr. Tamkin? But the novel itself – by critical consensus Bellow's most brilliantly crafted, and in many ways his most *representative* work[5] – invites the kind of speculative questioning with which this reading of *Seize the Day* begins. For the novel dramatizes contrasting styles of behavior, moral and economic, as it explores the complex psychological relationship between fathers and sons. In fact, one of the pressing issues *between* Dr. Adler and Tommy involves the matter of civility, of proper personal deportment. Dr. Adler, a "master of social behavior" (28) in Bellow's description, is repelled by the son's often manic gesturings, by Tommy's inability to control himself: "Dr. Adler felt that his son was indulging himself too much in his emotions" (47). Tommy's "problem," according to his socially self-conscious father, in other words, is that he "feels" too much; for Bellow, by contrast, Tommy's ability to feel is the prerequisite for personal freedom, the basis of his "bid for liberty" (25), not just from his unfeeling father, but from a constraining (Protestant) business culture that measures the self only by the outward signs of material success: money and style. In this respect *Seize the Day* situates itself as a work of substantial social criticism (ca. 1956) in commodity-conscious/obsessed America, limned by the teeming world of Manhattan's Upper West Side. As the novel follows Tommy's ordeal of material defeat and fatherly rejection, Bellow wishes us to understand that (at a deeper level of consciousness) Tommy is redeemed *through* his release of "uncivilized" emotion: Tommy's heartfelt tears at the end signal his moral victory over the rigid structures of affective restraint. His rush of feeling enables him to open a channel to the soul, the necessary passage to "overflowing comprehension"[6] – the moral activity that, in Bellow's imagination, makes us human.

In light of what might be called the discourse of manners, emotions, and civility in *Seize the Day*, my essay seeks to provide a fuller context for understanding the core themes explored in the novel. Why, I want to ask, does Dr. Adler feel so disgusted by Tommy's bad manners? (A correlative question: What is the deeper genealogy of this particular father-son divide itself?) Why does Bellow elevate emotion to a kind of cultural-expressive ideal? (Again, what is the genealogy of the affects that shapes Bellow's vision of emotion itself?) The answer to these (and other) issues generated by such a "contextualized" reading of *Seize the Day*, it turns out, involves situating the text within and against certain key cultural-social-psychological matrices related to immigrant Jewish experience.

Although *Seize the Day* makes passing reference to aspects of Jewish American life and Dr. Tamkin in his zany *luftmensch* aspect is a familiar figure out of Yiddish folklore,[7] the novel's relation to key dimensions of Jewish American culture may be distilled, first, from Bellow's own scattered but revealing pronouncements (along with one key story, "The Old System" [1967]) about his relation to immigrant Jewish experience, and second, by the larger cultural discourse of civility and manners that in many ways shaped the immigrants' experience itself. For *Seize the Day* emerges, from this perspective, as something of a *reverse* immigrant novel, where the traditional narrative of striving, new-world sons, embarrassed by the "barbaric" ways of their "greenhorn," old-world fathers is inverted: In *Seize the Day* old Dr. Adler represents new-world (economic) arrival and its intra-familial costs, whereas the pathetic Tommy, in his clownish behavior, reverts back to what Bellow calls the "old system" of Jewish (sometimes styled "Russian" or "East European") affections, "a real, genuine old Jewish type" that, as a character in *Herzog* observes, "digs the emotions."[8]

45

* * * * *

The encounter between the "old Jewish type" and American society proved both exhilarating and bewildering, especially for the new-world voyagers. By the early twentieth century, cities, especially New York, were overflowing with emigrants, mainly from Eastern Europe and the Russian Pale of Settlement. Bellow's own family arrived in Montreal during this huge wave of migration (he was born in Canada in 1915) and eventually settled in Chicago. From the beginning the shock of immigrant arrival stunned and vexed guardians of the dominant culture. Debate swirled among defenders and detractors of these "new" Americans. Henry James worried at the turn of the century about the dire, fatal impact the coarse urban tones of immigrant voices would have on the future of American speech. E. A. Ross, in his nativist attack on immigration, *The Old World in the New* (1914), wrote specifically of "the Jewish invader": "What is disliked in the Jews," Ross admitted, "is not their religion but certain ways and manners." As a result of a "tribal spirit intensified by social isolation" in Europe, "they use their Old-World *shove* and wile and lie in a society like ours . . . they rapidly *push up* into a position of prosperous parasitism, leaving scorn and curses in their wake" (emphasis added).[9]

Examples of nativist-antisemitic rant similar to Ross's – that the Jews shoved and pushed their way *into* genteel (gentile) America – were pervasive during the early years of this century. Nightmares of social and economic and sexual boundaries blurred and transgressed, fears of the American "stock" tainted by foreign blood, above all concern over the impact of perceived (or imagined) immigrant incivility on what sociologist John Murray Cuddihy terms "the Protestant etiquette" – all these cultural anxieties surfaced in the wake of early twentieth-century shocks to the national body politic.[10] With respect to Saul Bellow – and with him the generation of immigrant sons, many of whom (as Kramer notes in the introduction) became important public intellectuals and academics – his experience (and thus memory) of nativist scorn and attendant ethnic rivening proved crucial to his literary imagination. The sociological term for this strenuous encounter between the immigrant psyche and the "host" culture is "Americanization," the complex dynamic of personal and collective negotiation – rejection, appropriation, refashioning – in the process of new-world adjustment. The attendant strain, pain, and (especially in Bellow) comedy of Americanization forms the core subject of much Jewish American fiction and autobiography. Situated within and against this discourse – of immigrant fathers and intellectual sons, of provincial neighborhoods and the wider world, of "civilized" new-world language and incivil "Jewish" manners and emotion – *Seize the Day* can be read as a text which effectively *tropes* the traditions of immigrant narrative Bellow inherited.[11]

In numerous interviews, essays, and some of his fiction (notably in *Herzog*, but above all in "The Old System" – briefly analyzed below), Bellow has described in telling ways his feelings about the immigrant legacy. In "A Matter of the Soul" (1975) he speaks of growing up in "primordial Chicago": "We were the children of groping, baffled immigrants who were trying to figure out what had become of them in America. . . . Crudity, disappointment, sickness, heartbreak, money, power, happiness, and love in rudimentary forms – this was what we were aware of."[12] At the end of his Jefferson Lecture (1977), in part a jeremiad about the loss of "genial street life from American cities," Bellow invokes Henry James's *American Scene* (1907), in light of his own relation to James's worry about the fate of the American language: "When he visited the Lower East Side, James was alarmed by the Jewish immigrants he saw, appalled by their alien, ill-omened presence, their antics and their gabble. . . . There is no end to the curious ironies all this offers to an active imagination – and, in particular, to a descendant of East European Jews like myself."[13] In recalling his post-World War II sojourn in Paris, Bellow summons the James of *The American Scene* once again, this time confessing to an uneasiness about his own relation to "the Paris of Henry James": "I had my reservations also about the Paris of Henry James – bear in mind the unnatural squawking of East Side Jews as James described it in *The American Scene*. You wouldn't expect a relative of those barbarous East Siders to be drawn to the world of Madame de Vionnet [a main character in James's late novel, *The Ambassadors*], which had, in any case, vanished long ago'' (''My Paris'' [1983]).[14]

These striking reflections about Jewish American experience reveal how fiercely attached Bellow remains to the immigrant generation, indeed how spiritually invested he is as descendant of such baffled yet heroic fathers, despite the ironies inscribed in the son's (famous) progress toward proficiency in writing and speaking the English language (vide Bellow's Nobel Prize, the ultimate vindication against nativist anxieties about the ethnic debasing of the language). The descriptive tones bespeak Bellow's recognition of these rich ironies: ''groping,'' ''their antics and their gabble,'' ''unnatural squawking.'' Though pejorative, perhaps even shame-inducing when voiced by an awesome figure like Henry James (and other worried WASP observers of the immigrant urban ''swarm''), Bellow's ''active imagination'' transforms these marks of helpless new-world incivility into a rich linguistic patrimony. The *problem* of (immigrant) manners for the Protestant etiquette thus becomes Bellow's opportunity, and – given his early training in cultural anthropology under Melville Hershkovits – among his most frequently engaged subjects. The antics, gabbling, squawking, bewilderment, pain, heartbreak, and rudimentary love: all these (and more) ''primitive'' affects will eventually comprise the behavioral-expressive elements of what Bellow terms the immigrant Jewish ''opera'' – an extreme dramatization of the ethnic soul, fundamental in my view for an understanding of *Seize the Day* and Bellow's Jewish imagination in general – carried over in spiritual steerage from the *heart* of the Russian Pale.

The most profound evocation of this cultural-affective passage is Bellow's ''The Old System,'' a great story only now beginning to be appreciated as perhaps the key short text in the Bellow canon. ''I wrote 'The Old System' with all the stops out,' '' Bellow remarked in 1979. ''All that family feeling.''[15] It is a narrative filled, as its best recent critics have noted, with ''melodramatic excesses of the Jewish immigrant experience,'' of ''the expansive, volatile emotions that characterized immigrant Jewish life.'' Above all, ''The Old System'' recovers ''an enchanted immigrant moment" of tribal affections as it narrates the external and internal sagas of a family's "making it" in America.[16]

On the level of plot, "The Old System" chronicles the story of Isaac Braun and his extended family, a narrative mediated through the complex consciousness of his younger cousin Dr. Braun, a specialist in the "chemistry of heredity," who adheres to the authority of civility and reason, and who is jogged into deep remembrance, during a cold winter's day, about how years ago his older cousin Isaac successfully negotiated the Protestant business etiquette and amassed a huge personal fortune in upstate New York in the twenties and thirties.[17] That story stirs Dr. Braun to recall the ancient grievances within the family itself, tribal wounds involving Isaac's sister Tina and the delivery of a bribe ($100,000) to a local influential gentile businessman ("Old Ilkington") on the sale of country club land for future development. Isaac completes the transaction, surviving the ordeal of entering Ilkington's antiseptic world, with its "old goy taste," its "old goy odor," the encounter with "the pork-pale colors of gentility" ("System," 61; the repetition of "old" highlights the "newness" of Isaac's recent history in the promised land of America). All alone in this affectless new world, where "what you showed, among these people, you showed with silence" ("System," 73–4), Isaac feels "lost – lost to his people, his family, lost to God, lost in the void of America" ("System," 61).

Bellow releases "all the stops" by the end, presenting a vivid display of Jewish "opera" in airing this private, tribal narrative, which concerns the deathbed demand of sister Tina: she refuses to see her rich brother, against whom she has held an eternal grudge (he refused, in her view, to let the rest of the family in on the land deal; in truth, she blinked at the threshold of the payoff, choosing not to contribute her portion of the bribe), unless he now delivers $20,000 in person. (" 'A Jewish death bed scene, that's what he wants' " ["System," 70] she tells her husband, Mutt.) This chronicle of family crisis (the airing of "dirty laundry," in Daniel Fuchs's apt phrase),[18] and its larger meaning for the immigrant story in America forms the core of Dr. Braun's act of historical recuperation of "his dead" ("System," 64). Stung by her emotional blackmail, Isaac seeks the advice of an Ortho-dox rabbi in Brooklyn, after receiving no spiritual solace, or emo-tional outlet for his despair, in the restrained religious atmo-sphere of his own upstate congregation. Bellow/Dr. Braun conjures the new world/system of "restrained," *civilized*, modern piety: "Striking breasts with fist in old-fashioned penitence. The new way was the way of understatement. Anglo-Saxon restraint. The rabbi, with his Madison Avenue public-relations airs, did not go for these European Judaic, operatic fist-clenchings. Tears. He made the cantor tone it down" ("System," 69).

As one of those old-world Jews who "digs the emotions," a mythic figure from the immigrant generation still living on "the old system," Dr. Braun is moved by Isaac and his story into con-templating the fate of feeling in the new world, and his own relation, as a man of reason and science, to the immigrant legacy. "In Dr. Braun's opinion, his Cousin Tina had seized upon the force of death to create a situation of opera" ("System," 71). What claim does the operatic mode have on him? On Bellow? By the end of the story, Dr. Braun's suspended, liminal experi-ence of the past compels him to try to consider, to try "to grasp[,] what emotions were. What good were they! What were they for!" ("System," 82). For all his reliance on science and its cate-gorizing method (Dr. Braun continuously displays such a taxo-nomic strategy throughout the story), he is left stunned, bewil-dered, moved (up to a point), above all helpless before the Jewish "opera" he has recalled on this personal day of reckoning (or is it "atonement"?). "Oh these Jews – these Jews! Their feel-ings, their hearts! Dr. Braun wanted nothing more than to stop all this." But rudimentary feelings loosened by memory, dis-lodged by family pain, bring him an "intimation of understand-ing": "And these tears! When you wept them from the heart, you felt you justified something, understood something" ("Sys-tem," 83). The flow of tears, in Bellow's affective psychology, generates powers of empathy; emotion, specifically the uncon-tained feelings unleashed by the performance of "Jewish opera," enables the self to connect with the past, to recover the archaic sources of suffering and nobility that constitute our very identity as human beings. Such an encounter – an epiphany? – the creation of an open channel to the past – seems to be underway at the end of "The Old System," Bellow's brilliant rendering of the immigrant experience in America.

* * * * *

Dr. Braun is figured in "The Old System" as a representative of a later ("third") generation of Jews in America. He can "safely" contemplate ethnic family history (personal and collective) through the distancing lens of his scientific method. Such "toned down" negotiations, however, were far more difficult for the co-hort of immigrant sons of Bellow's own generation, a talented cohort whose immigrant patrimony proved at times a terrific burden, especially for those college-educated, intellectual sons of immigrant fathers who worshiped at the altar of American cul-ture (often, in fact, at the altar of Henry James!). This generation of Jewish American critics (dubbed the "New York Intellectuals" by Irving Howe) immediately appropriated Bellow as *their* nov-elist, the one artist who intimately transcribed their life stories, the one figure who truly understood their innermost affective worlds. (See Kramer's introduction.) Alfred Kazin, Bellow's exact contemporary who has written shrewdly about Bellow for over fifty years, recognized from the beginning that "the vitality of Bellow's fiction comes from the importance of being a Jewish son." "The sharp, questioning, exultingly self-educated mind of the immigrant's son is on every page" of Bellow's novels (nota-bly *The Adventures of Augie March* [1954]).[19]

The evocative narratives of two other famous Jewish sons of Bellow's generation also help in the process of situating a work like *Seize the Day*. Together, they highlight how that novel builds on, as it inverts, the received conventions of depicting genera-tional tension in Jewish American narrative. The first, "The Lost Young Intellectual," subtitled "A Marginal Man, Twice Alien-ated," is by the late Irving Howe, who at the age of 26 published this deeply personal essay in *Commentary*, in the fall of 1946; the second is *Passage from Home*, a novel by Bellow's very close friend, Isaac Rosenfeld, also published in 1946. In each case, the core – and power – of the narrative involve a complex negotiation with the immigrant past, which means a complex encounter with the immigrant fathers.[20]

Howe's essay concerns the palpable sense of loss, of cultural and self-estrangement that his (second) generational status in America confers upon the young Jew "detached" from the traditions and rituals of the faith. "His attitude [interestingly, Howe casts his memoir in the distancing third person] to the Jewish cultural tradition . . . is an ambiguous compound of rejection and nostalgia. . . . [he] exhibit[s] all of the restless, agonizing rootlessness that is the Jew's birthmark," despite the condition of marginality and detachment. Above all, Howe confesses, "*He has lost the sense of continuity which was such sustenance to his forefathers*" (emphasis in the original).[21] The primal scene depicting this filial rupture usually occurs in public, in the "Americanizing" spheres of the classroom and the street. As Howe relates these primordial traumas, it is the public *display* of the private, familiar (*heimisch*), heartfelt Yiddish – or a heavily Yiddish-inflected accent – that signals the son's irreversible alienation from the world of the Bronx fathers. In one traumatic scene (tellingly, Howe shifts into the first person to relate these still raw experiences), the young Irving Howe utters the Yiddish word for "fork" – *goopel* – in an imagined alert response to his kindergarten teacher's request to name that utensil (it was, after all, the first day of class, and Irving sought to impress his teacher with his knowledge of the world). His classmates laugh at his lapse (Yiddish-speaking children, they all know the difference between "fork" and "goopel"), and Howe vows never to speak Yiddish again. (Informing his parents of his decision, Howe recalls, "was a shock for them, the first in a series of conflicts between immigrant and America.")[22]

A more momentous occasion of rupture occurs when Irving cringes at being summoned home for dinner by his old-world shopkeeper father. Listen to the lost, young Jewish intellectual recount the trauma:

When I was a few years older, about eight or nine, my parents had a grocery store in an "Americanized" Jewish neighborhood, the West Bronx. I used to play in an abandoned lot about a block away from the store, and when I'd neglect to come home at supper time, my father would come to call for me. He would shout my name from afar, giving it a Yiddish twist: "Oivee!" I would always feel a sense of shame at hearing my name so mutilated in the presence of amused onlookers, and though I would come home – supper was always supper! – I would always run ahead of my father as if to emphasize the existence of a certain distance between us.[23]

This "primal" scene of alienation and shame leads to the heart of the generational abyss that forms the affective core of Jewish American (and perhaps all ethnic/immigrant) fiction, at least in the early twentieth century. Howe's father "squawks" (to recall Bellow's startling term for characterizing the abrasive immigrant tone) the name of the son before the "amused" eyes of the more "Americanized" – that is, *civilized* – world of the West Bronx. The son would like to disappear ("The aim of shame," observes psychoanalyst Léon Wurmser, "is invisibility"[24]), but all he can do is "run ahead," in a helpless gesture toward separation, conscious of the filial divide, a chasm marked by the barbaric "gabblings" of "East" (as opposed to "West") Bronx language, voice, and inflection (issues of class may also have played a part in Howe's youthful chagrin; by the late twenties the West Bronx symbolized upward mobility, the emerging middle class's escape from the Lower East Side). Only in retrospect does the son recognize the symbolic meaning of the shame-ridden effort at distancing; only later can he name it as a precursor to the collective "angst" of his generation, "a feeling," Howe relates, "that can be described as one of total loneliness, of complete rootlessness."[25]

As noted above, the theme of filial alienation and shame pervades Jewish American expression in the first half of this century, from the early cinema (especially in Edward Sloman's important *His People* [1925]), to Anzia Yezierska's stories of immigrant life, collected as *Children of Loneliness* (1923), Henry Roth's *Call It Sleep* (1934) – by consensus the most important novel about fathers and sons, the evocative power of immigrant speech, and the redemptive potential of the city in the canon of Jewish American literature (Bellow's major subjects, by the way!). Perhaps the most poignant portrait of these core themes is Isaac Rosenfeld's *Passage from Home* (1946), a neglected but richly suggestive work that also helps clarify some of the interpretive issues encountered in reading *Seize the Day*. Rosenfeld was among Bellow's most cherished friends growing up in Chicago, and in some respects a version of Tommy Wilhelm, if Tommy had studied philosophy instead of trying his luck in Hollywood. (Rosenfeld died still a young man of 38 in the year *Seize the Day* was published; in a personal reflection Bellow remarks that Rosenfeld "was a marvelous clown," and "preferred to have things about him in a mess"[26] as a personal protest against the conventions of middle-class cleanliness. More about the figures of Rosenfeld and Tommy Wilhelm as 1950s dissenters below.)

Without offering an extended analysis of *Passage from Home*, let me mention that the novel concerns the journey of a fastidious and sensitive young man, Bernard, into a new world of sensibility at odds with the traditional Jewish worlds of his father and grandfather. My interest in the figure of Bernard involves the way he feels about his "fathers," and the way he fashions himself against their ways of being. Above all, I am concerned with how – and why – Bernard is repulsed by the manners (table and personal) of his immigrant grandfather. In a crucial passage Bernard observes how, while in the public street, the patriarch devours his food: "I felt rather disgusted as I saw him tear out a deep, doughy chunk [of "bread smeared with chicken fat"], avoiding the crust, chewing with his mouth open and rolling the bread over his gums. He smeared his fingers on his beard, and wiped his hands on his jacket before drawing out a crusty handkerchief with which he dabbed at his lips."[27] (Similar scenes of shame and disgust fill the early cinema by the way.) Like an anthropologist observing the table manners of a primitive tribe (but without the "objectivity"), Bernard, as (grand)son, cannot tolerate the "barbarous" eating styles of the father(s), despite the pull, the "ecstatic" potential of orthodoxy represented by the spiritual fire of the pious older generation. He cannot tolerate this display of raw desire because he himself, as son, has become (or yearns to be) "civilized," identified with the world of manners and decorum he has chosen, indeed as the son of such "greenhorns" is *compelled* to embrace, as the distinguishing mark of his separation, perhaps his freedom from the old-world ways of being and eating.

But Bernard's revulsion at such unbuttoned gustatory display is only the obverse of a powerful need for order, for "restraint, the compulsion that kept me tidy . . . an endless inner house-keeping with no Sabbath in view," in Rosenfeld's astonishing description.[28] In effect, the obsession with table manners, with matters of civility, masks Bernard's own cultural self-hatred, to-gether with the unearned sense of "homelessness" he feels in-nately as a Jew. The powerful drama of *Passage from Home* details Bernard's journey from filial denial to filial feeling, especially toward his own father ("I was forever disappointed in my fa-ther,"[29] he confesses at the beginning of the novel). Bernard must learn to negotiate the dangerous territory of emotion, "to follow my father into the peril of intimacy,"[30] toward reconcilia-tion. Rather than remain in his safe position of remoteness, the intellectual son "cut off [from the father] by his own complex-ity" ("*He is a victim of his own complexity of vision*,"[31] Irving Howe declared, in 1946, of his generation's special fate), needs to re-connect, to breach the filial divide through what Bernard's father terms "absolute trust in each other. . . . We should be absolutely open with each other." Alas, the dream of generational truce remains ambiguous, unrealized, by the end of *Passage from Home*; despite Bernard's recognition that he desperately needs his father – "nothing I did," he is at last able to admit, "was truly indepen-dent of his [life], if only because, to find pleasure in selfishness – I could not bear to be alone – I clung to him, needing the knowl-edge and the assurance of his nearness. My love was my guilt" – he remains burdened with the consciousness of his inability to love, his inability to live without illusion. "Now there would only be life as it came and the excuses one made to himself for ac-cepting it."[32]

"Isaac was out for the essential qualities," Bellow points out in his warm portrait of Rosenfeld. "He believed that heart and truth were to be had."[33] The same desire for "openness of heart," the same yearning "for the essential qualities" might be said to characterize Bellow's own aesthetic-moral vision, as well as perfectly describe Tommy Wilhelm, the Jewish son in terrible financial and spiritual trouble. But for all his "alienation" from the grasping, commodity-obsessed world of the 1950s, Tommy is decidedly not a young, lost, alienated, New York intellectual, like the young Irving Howe; he may be among "the most watchful of Jewish sons," as Kazin once described his friend Saul Bellow, but Tommy cannot eloquently articulate the condition of his marginality, either to the world of the fathers, or to the culture at large. Tommy cannot transform the conflicted condition of "rejection and nostalgia" (Howe) into art, as does Rosenfeld in *Passage from Home*. Rather than being able to analyze his particular burden, Tommy can only *express* it; he's a *schlemiel* who feels.[34]

In reality, Tommy Wilhelm is something of an easily distracted, helpless Jewish son, struggling to get a grip on his shaky middle-aged existence. But we should not convict Tommy for his apparent lack of thin *intellectual* culture or for his limited self-consciousness. Most college students, reading *Seize the Day* for the first time, tend to bristle at Wilhelm's apparent personal inertia, his seeming inability to change his life. They voice their exasperation by screaming at him to "get a life!," to "do something!" No one, I suspect, wants to admit to personal and professional failure at any age; and young college students, all dreaming at the threshold of great careers, would prefer (naturally) not to gaze into the depressing (distorting?) mirror held up by the figure of Tommy Wilhelm. So what claim does Wilhelm have on us? On Bellow? Why should we care about his particular fate?[35]

My answer to this question begins with a close reading of the way Bellow renders the ancient tensions between Dr. Adler and his son, and how their archaic antagonisms resonate in light of the discourses of manners and civility that (in my view) shaped the immigrant Jewish experience in America.

When we first meet Tommy, he is worried – "mainly for his old father's sake" (3) – about his appearance; his strenuous effort at *appearing* psychically and physically at ease, his quest for calm in the midst of personal upheaval prove hopeless, futile, for Tommy cannot stand (or sit) still. He is restless, agitated, consumed with a nameless, nervous "energy" that he cannot discharge. By contrast, Dr. Adler is a model of self-containment. Unlike his son, the Doctor makes "no stupid gesture[s]" (11), "he liked to appear affable" (10), his tones are "low-voiced, tasteful" (11), his voice "precise" (30). "A master of social behavior''(28), Dr. Adler ''behaved toward his son as he had formerly done toward his patients'' – to the ''great grief'' of Tommy. ''Couldn't he see – couldn't he feel? Had he lost his family sense?'' (11) Tommy wonders, as he laments his condition of estrangement and personal shame.

These questions announce the complex generational divide that shapes the drama of *Seize the Day*. Matters of feeling, matters of family are the ultimate issues at stake here, but in his policy of absolute decorum Dr. Adler remains adamantly blocked, either to the display of feeling or the recollection of family history. Wilhelm is blocked as well, his roiling emotions pent up, seeking release (''He hadn't been able to get rid of his energy'' [7][36]). In its movement and structure, *Seize the Day* works toward the release of all that Tommy has repressed, which includes fragments of poetry once deeply felt, the true meaning of his relationship with his father, and above all his need to connect, to be moved by, and to move, other people. ''Dad,'' Tommy thinks to himself, in a crucial moment of recognition, ''I couldn't affect one way or another'' (15). It's a brilliant flash of insight, revealing (however briefly) his father's *affectless* style and his own efforts (born of love) to adjust Dr. Adler's habitual aloofness.

The problem is that, for the father, Tommy embodies all that Dr. Adler seeks to repress, to deny in himself. When he observes, cool clinician that he always is, his son's behavior, he is disgusted, repelled by Tommy's bad manners. The residue of grime that Tommy's dirty fingers leave on the white eggshell at breakfast confirms Dr. Adler in his rejection. He cannot tolerate – neither stomach nor swallow – how Tommy lives (in sublime filth, using the red plastic seals of cigarette packs as makeshift dental floss, randomly tossing garbage into the back seat of his car); he cannot understand Tommy's chronic fidgeting (''Why the devil can't he stand still when we're talking? He's either hoisting his pants up and down by the pockets or jittering his feet. A regular mountain of tics he's getting to be,'' Dr. Adler thinks to himself, observing Tommy's ''antics'' [27–8]); most tellingly, Dr. Adler cannot bear Tommy's embarrassing habit of gesticulating.[37]

In perhaps the key scene between father and son, Tommy starts to strangle himself, in order to dramatize for his affectless father his current feelings of helplessness and despair (really, to demonstrate what his wife, who refuses to grant him a divorce, is doing to him):

> Wilhelm took hold of his broad throat with brown-stained fingers and bitten nails and began to choke himself.
> "What are you doing?" cried the old man.
> "I'm showing you what she does to me."
> "Stop that – stop it!" the old man said and tapped the table commandingly. (48)

During the same exchange, dumbfounded by his father's incapacity to listen to his plight, Tommy "struggle[s] for breath and frown[s] in his father's face":

> "I don't understand your problems," said the old man. "I never had any of them."
> By now Wilhelm had lost his head and he *waved his hands* and said over and over, "Oh, Dad, don't give me that stuff, don't give me that. Please don't give me that sort of thing."
> "It's true," said the father. "I come from a different world. Your mother and I led an entirely different life."
> "Oh, how can you compare Mother," Wilhelm said. "Mother was a help to you. Did she harm you, ever?"
> *"There's no need to carry on like an opera,* Wilky . . . This is only your side of things." (49, emphasis added)

Tommy, we might say, speaks from the heart in this exchange. His histrionic behavior is expressive of the old system, the old Jewish mode of "operatic" feeling.[38] In demanding that the son tone down his "silly" behavior, to act with civility, the father betrays his own anxieties, exposing the roots of his disgust toward his hapless son.

The commandment against public display is laced with ironies, in light of the exchange at breakfast with Mr. Perls. Discussing family history, Dr. Adler claims that *he* represents "tradition": "I uphold tradition," he explains to those who ask, in the context of Tommy's change of name from Adler to Wilhelm; "He's for the new" (14). But at the level of affective style and the religion of the heart it's just the opposite. Tommy Wilhelm – the name change signals his conscious bid for liberty, a way to deliver himself from the father's strategy of keeping him a "small son" (11), a "Wilky" (note how the father invokes that archaic name to "tone down" Tommy's operatic gestures, which shame him, the father, into memory) – represents the grand traditions of the Jewish opera which his father labors to repress. Why does Dr. Adler resist discussing family history (especially his married life)? Because Tommy conjures, by his extravagant behavior, the living presence of his mother: "From his mother he had gotten sensitive feelings, a soft heart, a brooding nature, a tendency to be confused under pressure" (25). In short, Tommy's maternal inheritance returns the repressed, affective world of the past, both his own family's and the larger Jewish past of immigrant experience – the buried realm of the primordial. In this respect Tommy's "truest" name may indeed be "Velvel," his deeper identity inscribed by the *mamaloshen* (mother-tongue) Yiddish, uttered by the grandfather(s). Thus Tommy still remembers, as Bellow sketches his hero's spiritual biography, how his mother "tried to stop me, and we carried on and yelled and pleaded" (15; an intimation of Adler family opera?) when he decided to start out in the thirties by making a new beginning in Hollywood. For all the wonderfully comic dimension of the scenes with the "talent" scout Maurice Venice, we should note that he at least senses some enabling potential about Wilhelm, a possibility of self that Bellow (I believe) wants us to recognize as well: "Let yourself go. . . . Don't be afraid to make faces and be emotional. Shoot the works. . . . You don't behave the same way as the average" (22). The advice touches the source of Tommy's deepest desires: "to be freed from the anxious and narrow life of the average" (23). Acting thus becomes an outlet for his substantial reservoirs of affect, letting go – the "gesture" (Bellow's key word; gestures/gesturing lead us to the soul) of becoming "Tommy Wilhelm" – as his/the heart's ultimate need, in contrast to his father's labor of self-mastery, his effort at social control. Venice's injunctions thus implicitly oppose the commandments of the father; and Tommy, in search of personal validation unavailable at home, grasps at the talent scout's ego-nourishing promise, however insubstantial, of Hollywood.

Thus Tommy, through his inheritance of his mother's emotionally receptive line, *embodies* the ''old system'' of immigrant Jewish opera; and this genealogy of the heart gives him access to realms of feeling, or the potential of feeling proscribed by the implicitly WASP-identified world of reserved Dr. Adler. Tommy's ''channels'' of emotion are blocked, in part by the father's authority, in part by the overbearing urban scene of New York City in the 1950s, in part by the cult of success *against which* Tommy's behavior looms as an implicit critique.[39] In subtle ways, Tommy's ''pathology'' (if we can term his behavior pathological) comments on the ''Americanizing'' process itself (Dr. Adler and rapacious Mr. Rappaport are its symbols). Can we say, with some recent psychoanalytic theorists, that Tommy's symptoms reveal ''the parents' repressed doubts about their own ideals and ambitions''?[40] Does Tommy's unconscious quest for affective bonding with all of humanity – the axial lines of democratic solidarity tugging at him in the subway – expose the father's guilty embrace of the American mania for success? (In other moments of insight, Tommy sees through the cult, recognizing the deformations wrought by the money culture.) At some level, Tommy's ''symptoms'' provide an indirect critique, both of the ''heartless'' commodity-obsessed 1950s and of Americanization itself, a culturally attenuating process which distills all vibrant traces of ethnic/immigrant residues in the ordeal of achieving WASP ''civility and manners.'' The cautionary tale of such a denaturing procedure is Dr. Adler himself, whom Bellow tellingly describes as ''a rather bland old man'' (10; he is continuously abstracted as ''an old man'' in the verbal exchanges with Tommy, not as ''a father'' – the implication being that ''America'' has drained him of any and all ''fatherly'' attributes: ''The fathers were no fathers'' [84]).

On the matter of psychoanalysis, and of Freudian modes of therapy in general, Bellow has been outspoken, for the most part critical.[41] In this respect the character of Dr. Tamkin represents Bellow's wicked satire on the obsession with therapeutic styles (emerging as very popular, especially among angst-ridden [Jewish] intellectuals in the 1950s). As noted above, critics tend to view Tamkin as a figure out of Yiddish folklore, a flighty character whose office is ''in his socks'' (the reference is to Bernard

Malamud's great story, "The Magic Barrel"); but whatever he is, he succeeds as a self-styled therapist of the soul offering succor to Tommy, who is in desperate need of any attention – and affection ("This was what he craved, that someone should care about him, wish him well. Kindness, mercy, he wanted" [73]). Tamkin may not provide mercy, but he does help Tommy in his journey toward the soul by distracting him from the troubling business with his father and by relieving the constant pressure building inside Tommy through the therapy of laughter. Above all, Tamkin's words – and the quack therapist is one of Bellow's great talkers – "caught Wilhelm's heart" (71); his words tug at Tommy where it counts, enabling him to reconnect with words (notably fragments of poems that continue to resonate in his heart). In part through Tamkin's therapeutic office Tommy begins to comprehend what Bellow calls "the peculiar burden" (56) of his existence, to carry a heavy load of feeling (Tamkin?), for himself – Tommy learns to take pity on himself rather than wallow in self-hatred (the self-castigating, father-imposed "Wilky" aspect of the self) – and for mankind in general.

This redemptive realm of the soul always remains active for Bellow, but it tends to be blocked by the thickets of civility, by the modern cult of emotional aloofness (recall Dr. Braun's late-day meditations). "There were depths in Wilhelm," "some remote element in his thoughts," Bellow informs us, in what is perhaps the most important passage in *Seize the Day*, where he receives the intimation "that the business of life, the real business – to carry his peculiar burden, to feel shame and impotence, to taste these quelled tears – the only important business, the highest business was being done" (56). Dr. Tamkin points Tommy toward this realm of consciousness by helping *banish* the figure of the father: "The sight of Dr. Tamkin brought his quarrel with his father to a close. He found himself flowing into another channel" (57). Tamkin, who speaks "a kind of truth" (63), opens a necessary channel to the soul; in the case of Tommy Wilhelm, the channel opens out into general, Whitmanesque "involuntary feelings" (85) for the crowds of Manhattan.[42] On this, his "day of reckoning" (96; or is it his true Day of Atonement?), Tommy allows the cumulative emotional blockage to break through, to let go; his blockage flows into breakthrough as he mourns for himself, crying "with all his heart" (118).

Much has been written about the closing epiphany of *Seize the Day*, with some critics arguing for its brilliant aptness (in light of the metaphoric resonances in the pattern of water imagery, the movement toward catharsis, and so forth) whereas others find Tommy's effusive release ambiguous, and thus the novel's attempt at closure problematic. Rather than enter that debate, let me suggest that the famous scene of mourning and release resembles, in light of the genealogy of manners and emotions I have attempted to outline, an uncanny scene of Jewish "opera." For it turns out that unhinged, unalloyed (Jewish) feeling provides, in Bellow's metaphysics, a pure channel leading to the soul.

* * * * *

Beyond the forces of repression symbolized by the dominant culture, no longer heeding the father's injunction against emotion (Dr. Adler speaks on behalf of that culture), Tommy allows his feelings to flow, uncontained:

> Standing a little apart, Wilhelm began to cry. He cried at first softly and from sentiment, but soon from deeper feeling. He sobbed loudly and his face grew distorted and hot, and the tears stung his skin. . . . Soon he was past words, past reason, coherence. He could not stop. The source of all tears had suddenly sprung open within him, black, deep, and hot, and they were pouring out and convulsed his body, bending his stubborn head, bowing his shoulders, twisting his face, crippling the very hands with which he held the handkerchief. (117–18)

To my own attentive ears, I hear operatic notes sounding, swelling through this description; Tommy sobs "loudly," his face registers the extremity of released emotion: "grew distorted," his "convulsed" body, his "crippled" hands no longer under rational control. One can perhaps hear as well old Dr. Adler rebuking the son to tone down his behavior – "There's no need [Wilky] to carry on like an opera." Bellow, however, welcomes Tommy's convulsions, a type of those "European Judaic, operatic *fist-clenchings*. Tears," to summon Tommy's cousin across generations, the figure of Isaac Braun.[43]

In an even more complicated way Bellow would claim that Tommy's tears, his cosmic confusion, like Herzog's, are "barbarous." Writing just over ten years ago, in "The Civilized Barbarian Reader," Bellow spoke of Herzog's need to "return . . . to some primal point of balance," a zone of elemental connectedness sought after the failure of all systems of belief, of education, of civilization to help him cope with the confusions of the modern world. "Herzog's confusion is barbarous," Bellow explained. "Well, what else can it be?" "In the greatest confusion," Bellow continues, in something of a moral-aesthetic manifesto:

> there is still an open channel to the soul. It may be difficult to find because by midlife it is overgrown, and some of the wildest thickets that surround it grow out of what we call our education. But the channel is always there, and it is our business to keep it open, to have access to the deepest part of ourselves – to that part of us which is conscious of a higher consciousness, by means of which we make final judgments, and put everything together.[44]

At the end of *Seize the Day* Tommy Wilhelm gains access to the deepest registers of the self. His "barbarous confusion" in the noisy Babel/babble of the choking, smoke-filled city proves ultimately to be a means of spiritual redemption, for his (unconscious?) habit of emotion helps him break through the empty, impotent (recall the last image of the father, limp in the lower depths of the Gloriana hotel) civility that his *new-world* father employs in defense against dangerous emotion. Tommy and his nervous antics may resemble those of a textbook neurotic; he may be in desperate need of "empathic mirroring"[45]; he may be the pathetic *schlemiel* we would all prefer not to recognize in the mirror. But in the end Tommy's operatic mode of being exposes the blandness, the dis-ease of pork-pale civility; his symptoms critique and challenge the cult of (1950s) success. In the end Tommy's "barbarous confusion," a symptomatic response to the American world at mid-century, links him implicitly to the immigrant past of the emotional Jewish fathers (and mothers), his "gesture"/gesticulations expressive of a necessary process of becoming. "Having love," Irving Howe observed (years after his youthful confession of alienation), of the world of Sholem Aleichem's old-world *shtetl*, "they had no need for politeness."[46] Love versus politeness; enabling emotions versus artificial manners; redemptive barbarism versus repressive civility. In *Seize the Day* Tommy rediscovers, recuperates the old (world) system of the heart; and in the process he recovers, in Bellow's ultimate vision of personal success, indeed of personal salvation, a "primal point of balance."[47]

NOTES

1 Saul Bellow, "The Trip to Galena," *Partisan Review* 17 (1950): 789. This important early story, announced as part of a novel which Bellow never published, transcribes an intense exchange between Weyl, a patient hospitalized for depression (the voice of the epigraph) and his empathetic (empathic?) interlocutor Scampi. "The Trip to Galena" anticipates some of the core themes engaged by this essay, as the following passage suggests. Looking attentively at the unhinged Weyl, Bellow's narrator has Scampi make the following observations: "He sized him up, in his civilized heart as half-finished, original, eccentric, powerful, drugged by the effort of self-direction, in some ways tolerant, some ways overbearing, rough, barbarian, with learning unassimilated. And really impassioned. Really a man of feeling, though to define these feelings of his was a far larger project than Scampi had at first imagined." The discourses of civility, feeling, and the human heart will, in my view, become crucial for an understanding of *Seize the Day*.

2 Alfred Kazin, *A Lifetime Burning in Every Moment: From the Journals of Alfred Kazin* (New York: HarperCollins, 1996), p. 327.

3 Saul Bellow, *Herzog* (New York: Viking Press, 1964), p. 20.

4 These key phrases are taken from Saul Bellow, "The Distracted Public" (1990), in Bellow, *It All Adds Up: From the Dim Past to the Uncertain Future* (New York: Penguin Books), p. 168.

5 Most recently, Sanford Pinsker describes *Seize the Day* as "arguably Bellow's tightest, most perfectly executed fiction." Pinsker, "Saul Bellow: 'What, in all of this, speaks for man?' " *Georgia Review* 49 (1995): 90–1.

6 Bellow, ''The Distracted Public,'' p. 168.

7 On the subject of Bellow's relation to the traditions of Yiddish literature see Ruth R. Wisse, *The Schlemiel as Modern Hero* (Chicago: University of Chicago Press, 1971), chapter six, and Bellow's Introduction to his edition of *Great Jewish Short Stories* (New York: Dell Books, 1963).

8 Bellow, *Herzog*, p. 84.

9 Edward A. Ross, *The Old World in the New: The Significance of Past and Present Immigration to the American People* (New York: The Century Co., 1914), pp. 164, 154. Henry James worried about the immigrant challenge to American speechways in ''The Question of Our Speech'' (1905).

10 Compare John Murray Cuddihy, *The Ordeal of Civility: Freud, Marx, Levi-Strauss, and the Jewish Struggle with Modernity* (New York: Dell, 1974), p. 4. Cuddihy briefly treats Bellow in terms of the Jewish encounter with modernity on pp. 217–21.

11 Sabine Haenni speaks of Bellow's ''*troping* on the ethnic story'' in his earlier novel *The Victim* (1949) in a graduate seminar paper at the University of Chicago.

12 Bellow, *It All Adds Up*, p. 74.

13 Ibid., pp. 145, 152.

14 Ibid., p. 234.

15 ''Free to Feel: Conversation with Saul Bellow'' (1979) in *Conversations with Saul Bellow*, ed. Gloria L. Cronin and Ben Siegel (Jackson, MI: University Press of Mississippi, 1994), p. 163. Keith Opdahl ''is struck by how many of Bellow's attitudes belong to the Jewish immigrant experience. . . . the most striking influence of Jewish culture on a writer such as Bellow must be the emotional openness of his style.'' This essay draws out the implications of Opdahl's sharp observation. See Keith Opdahl, ''The 'Mental Comedies' of Saul Bellow,'' in *From Hester Street to Hollywood: The Jewish-American Stage and Screen*, ed. Sarah Blacher Cohen (Bloomington: Indiana University Press, 1983), p. 186.

16 Pinsker, ''Saul Bellow,'' p. 93; Daniel Fuchs, *Saul Bellow: Vision and Revision* (Durham, N. C.: Duke University Press, 1984), p. 298. One of the strongest recent readings of ''The Old System'' is Gregory Johnson, ''Jewish Assimilation and Codes of Manners in Saul Bellow's 'The Old System,' '' *Studies in American Jewish Literature* 9 (1990): 48–60.

17 Saul Bellow, ''The Old System'' (1967), in *Mosby's Memoirs and Other Stories* (New York: Fawcett World Library, 1969), p. 58. Sub-

sequent citations noted as *System* in the text. Interestingly, "The Old System" appeared in *Playboy* in 1967.

18 Fuchs, *Saul Bellow*, p. 298.

19 Alfred Kazin, *Bright Book of Life: American Novelists and Storytellers from Hemingway to Mailer* (New York: Dell Publishing Co. 1973), p. 134; Alfred Kazin, "The World of Saul Bellow" (1959), in Kazin, *Contemporaries* (Boston: Little, Brown, 1962), p. 219.

20 As Howe recounts it in his intellectual autobiography *A Margin of Hope*, his shock of recognition on reading – and subsequently re-viewing – Rosenfeld's novel led him to write, almost immediately, his own interpretation of the tortured passage out, from the Bronx to the wider world. See Irving Howe, *A Margin of Hope* (New York: Harcourt Brace Jovanovitch, 1982), pp. 112–14. Interestingly, Howe remembers the original title as the "alienated" rather than "lost" Jewish intellectual (p. 114).

21 Irving Howe, "The Lost Young Intellectual," *Commentary* 2 (Oct. 1946): 361, 362. For a helpful discussion of Howe's youthful essay, along with shrewd analyses of Rosenfeld, Bellow, and the general intellectual-political-psychological milieu of the "New York Intellectuals" see Mark Shechner, *After the Revolution: Studies in the Contemporary Jewish-American Imagination* (Bloomington: Indiana University Press, 1987), esp. pp. 16–7, 201–2.

22 Howe, "The Lost Young Intellectual," p. 364.

23 Howe, "The Lost Young Intellectual," p. 364. Almost forty years later, in his intellectual autobiography *A Margin of Hope*, Howe revisits this traumatic scene in this way: "As a boy, when I played in the streets too long, my father would come from his grocery store, wearing a white apron, to find me. He would shout 'Oivie,' and his pronunciation of my unloved name, together with his apron, so embarrassed me that I would run home ahead of him, as if to keep a distance. Half a century later, I still feel the shame." Howe, *A Margin of Hope*, p. 114.

24 Léon Wurmser, *The Mask of Shame* (Baltimore: The Johns Hopkins University Press, 1981), p. 84. "Shame anxiety," Wursmer observes, "is accompanied by a profound estrangement from world and self, present and past" (p. 53). The relations between shame affects and immigrant culture form the key matrix for Howe's particular experience as well as for much "ethnic" expression in general.

25 Howe, "The Lost Young Intellectual," 366.

26 Bellow, "Isaac Rosenfeld" (1956), in *It All Adds Up*, p. 265. The best

introduction to Rosenfeld's career and importance is by Shechner, *After the Revolution*, pp. 102–20.

27 Isaac Rosenfeld, *Passage from Home* (Cleveland: World Publishing, 1961 [1946]), p. 86. On the figure of Rosenfeld see Mark Shechner, "Introduction," *Passage from Home* (New York: Marcus Wiener Publishing, 1988), pp. i–xx; Mark Shechner, ed., *Preserving the Hunger: An Isaac Rosenfeld Reader* (Detroit: Wayne State University Press, 1988); and James Atlas's very helpful essay "Golden Boy," *The New York Review of Books* (June 29, 1989): 42–6.

28 Rosenfeld, *Passage from Home*, p. 126.

29 Ibid., p. 7.

30 Ibid., p. 280.

31 Ibid., p. 160; Howe, "Lost Young Intellectual," p. 366.

32 Rosenfeld, *Passage from Home*, pp. 277, 274, 280.

33 Bellow, *It All Adds Up*, p. 266.

34 Howe, "Lost Young Intellectual," p. 361; Kazin, *Bright Book of Life*, p. 132. In describing Tommy, I borrow from Irving Howe's 1968 introduction to *Seize the Day*: "Tommy is a slob who feels, a *shlemiehl* who struggles to understand his failure." Irving Howe, "Introduction to *Seize the Day*, in Howe, ed. *Classics of Modern Fiction* (New York: Harcourt Brace: 1968), p. 516. Interestingly, both Howe and Kazin have written passionately both about *Seize the Day* and in defense of Tommy Wilhelm. See Kazin's wonderful 1968 Introduction to *Seize the Day* (New York: Fawcett, 1968), pp. v–xxviii. The edition appears in the Fawcett "Masterworks Series," under the general editorship of Irving Howe.

35 I invoke these questions raised by Howe and Kazin, in their respective introductions to *Seize the Day*. See especially Kazin, p. xii: "What, then, sustains our interest in this non-hero? What makes him an interesting contender with life? What lifts him for a moment above our thick urban swarm, so that we *can* identify with him and finally mourn him as he mourns himself?"

36 Tommy's unchanneled energy, his compulsive restlessness, is often explained by the influence of the psycho-sexual speculations of psychoanalyst/theorist Wilhelm Reich. For an analysis of Reich's impact upon Bellow in the 1950s (Reich also deeply influenced Rosenfeld) see Eusebio Rodrigues, "Reichianism in *Seize the Day*," in *Critical Essays on Saul Bellow*, ed. Stanley Trachtenberg (Boston: G. K. Hall, 1979), pp. 89–100. For Reich's general influence on Jewish intellectuals in the '40s and '50s see Shechner, *After the Revolution*, pp. 91–101. ("Bellow absorbed the Reichian system in-

tact into the scheme of character analysis in two novels, *Seize the Day* and *Henderson the Rain King* [1959)]" p. 100.)

37 To cite just one of numerous examples of Tommy's "problematic" behavior: His father would not ride in the car with him, not only because it was filled with "waste paper and Coca-Cola bottles," but because while driving Tommy "dreamed at the wheel or argued or gestured . . . the old doctor would not ride with him" (34).

38 In this context Earl Rovit's general observation about Bellow's heroes, made *before* "The Old System," seems particularly apt: "Bellow's heroes suffer intensely and rehearse their agonies at operatic volume for all to hear." Earl Rovit, *Saul Bellow* (Minneapolis: University of Minnesota Press, 1967), p. 12.

39 For a number of critics, *Seize the Day* represents Bellow's substantial social criticism of the business economy, both in the 1950s and in our own time. The most recent exposition of this perspective is by Lee Siegel, "Ozick Seizes Bellow," *The Nation* (February 26, 1996): 34–6. Siegel is responding to an essay by Cynthia Ozick (one of Bellow's best critics) about *Seize the Day* and "the old system" of (high) literary culture: See Ozick, "Saul Bellow's Broadway," in *Fame and Folly* (New York: Alfred. A. Knopf, 1996), pp. 171–84.

40 Adam Phillips, "On Success," in *On Flirtation* (Cambridge, Mass.: Harvard University Press, 1994), p. 46.

41 For Bellow's stringent critique of Freudian theory as "system" see "Literature and Culture: An Interview with Saul Bellow," *Salmagundi* 30 (Summer 1975): 18–19. For a rich, important consideration of this issue see Daniel Fuchs, "Bellow and Freud," *Studies in the Literary Imagination* 17 (1984): 59–80. In the early 1960s Bellow wrote a play attempting to satirize psychoanalysis; see *The Last Analysis* (New York: The Viking Press, 1965).

42 Interestingly, Bernard Miller in *Passage from Home* gains an equivalent epiphany on the streets of his Chicago: "The whole world was involved in my particular quest, just as I was involved with the world. All these people here on the street seemed to be part of me, and I was part of them. . . . so I, too, expanding, dissolved and lost myself until I seemed no longer to exist in my own awareness." Rosenfeld, *Passage from Home*, p. 115.

43 Ten years later, in the famous 1966 *Paris Review* interview, Bellow discussed the question of "feeling" and literary style, and his own relation to the WASP literary-cultural establishment. Speaking of Russian writers, Bellow observed that "Their conventions allow them to express freely their feelings about nature and human be-

ings. We have inherited a more restricted and imprisoning attitude toward the emotions. We have to work around Puritanical and stoical restraint ["old goy style"]. We lack the Russian [that is, "Jewish"/old system] openness." Speaking personally, Bellow explained his own struggle with that "Wasp world"; "I was afraid to let myself go." Indeed, "as a son of immigrants, I could not . . . express a variety of things I knew intimately. . . . It was made clear to me when I studied literature in the university that as a Jew and the son of Russian Jews [key explanatory adjective] I would probably never have the right *feeling* for Anglo-Saxon traditions, for English words" (emphasis in original). "The Art of Fiction XXXVII Saul Bellow: An Interview," *Paris Review* #36 (1966): pp. 54, 55, 56. This confession/revelation highlights, as it explains, a number of issues, from Bellow's subsequent, self-conscious invocation of Henry James ("The Question of Our Speech") in light of his *Russian* immigrant origins to the crucial role of *feelings* in Bellow's metaphysics. The gentile literary world repressed Bellow's desire to express himself; finally, in 1954, he let himself go in *The Adventures of Augie March*. Thus, when Tommy Wilhelm, in a moment of self-insight, understands that "Feeling got me in dutch at Rojax. I had the *feeling* that I belonged to the firm, and my *feelings* were hurt when they put Gerber in over me" (56, emphasis in original), he is undergoing the prelude to the key Bellovian, operatic epiphany at the end of the novel – which culminates in an overflow of (Russian/Jewish) feeling. In another context, Irving Howe speaks of the "rudeness" of the New York Intellectuals. "Rudeness," he recalled in *A Margin of Hope*, "becomes a spear with which to break the skin of complacency. . . . Rudeness [he continues, with reference to the *Partisan Review* crowd] was not only the weapon of cultural underdogs, but also a sign that intellectual Jews had become sufficiently self-assured to stop playing by gentile rules. At the least, this rudeness was to be preferred to the frigid 'civility' with which English intellectuals cloak their murderous impulses, or the politeness that in American academic life can mask a cold indifference." *Margin of Hope*, p. 140. For the larger cultural contexts for rudeness as a strategy of critique and revenge, see Cuddihy, *The Ordeal of Civility*.

44 Saul Bellow, "The Civilized Barbarian Reader," *The New York Times Book Review* (March 8, 1987): 38. In perhaps the most stringent recent critique of Bellow's literary career, Bruce Bawer offers the following dissent on Bellow's entire achievement in terms, tellingly, of emotions: "Feelings in Bellow's novels are more often

named than believably communicated, more often discussed than truly felt." Bruce Bawer, "Talking Heads: The Novels of Saul Bellow," *The New Criterion* 6 (Sept., 1987): 10. Bawer, however, does call *Seize the Day* "Bellow's most admirable work of fiction – concise, cogent, and finely controlled" (14). Note, however, the striking contrast between the critic's admiration for "controlled" "form" (genteel literary establishment) and the striking "uncontrolled" behavior of the novel's hero (ethnic-emotional opera). In perhaps the toughest early critique of Bellow, Richard Poirier dissents on the achievement of *Herzog*, speaking of the "pseudo-philosophical or sociological or historical expansions of the otherwise parochial situations of [Bellow's] heroes." Richard Poirier, "Bellows to Herzog," *Partisan Review* 32 (1965): 267. Reflecting years later on his dissent, Poirier speaks of the "random vulgarity in the superficial notations" of certain (now famous) passages – decrying modernist alienation – in the novel. Richard Poirier, "Herzog, or, Bellow in Trouble," in *Saul Bellow: A Collection of Critical Essays*, ed. Earl Rovit (Englewood Cliffs, N.J.: Prentice-Hall, 1975), p. 82.

45 *Seize the Day* has received a number of psychological readings, most notably Daniel Weiss, "Caliban on Prospero: A Psychoanalytic Study on the Novel *Seize the Day*, by Saul Bellow," in *Psychoanalysis and American Fiction*, ed. Irving Malin (New York: E. P. Dutton, 1965), pp. 279–308; and more recently, J. Brooks Bouson, "The Narcissistic Self-Drama of Wilhelm Adler: A Kohutian Reading of Bellow's *Seize the Day*," *Saul Bellow Journal* 5 (1986): 3–14. See also the essay by Sam Girgus that follows mine in this volume.

46 Irving Howe, "Sholom Aleichem: Voice of Our Past," in Howe, *A World More Attractive: A View of Modern Literature and Politics* (New York: Horizon Press, 1963), p. 215. Howe's title suggests that he eventually discovered the answer to his youthful individual angst and alienation in the implicitly collective world of Yiddishkeit.

47 Bellow, "The Civilized Barbarian Reader," p. 38.

4

Imaging Masochism and the Politics of Pain: "Facing" the Word in the Cinetext of *Seize the Day*

SAM B. GIRGUS

THE IMAGE of Saint Sebastian as painted by Mantegna graces the cover of Kaja Silverman's *Male Subjectivity at the Margins*, an important and original study of masochism's power to complicate and multiply representations of masculinity in cinema, literature, and society. Bloodied arrows pierce his tormented body. His eyes and face appeal to heaven. This search for love and recognition from an invisible but omniscient deity suggests his pleasure in pain and suffering. So passive to physical abuse and so eager for fatherly approbation, the saint does not advance any traditional model of manly aggression or power.

However, the painting of Saint Sebastian on the cover of Silverman's *Male Subjectivity* personifies the mental state and character of Tommy Wilhelm, the miserably masochistic protagonist in Saul Bellow's *Seize the Day*. Moreover, Silverman's study of masochism and multiple masculinities in film and literature provides a useful model for analyzing both the literary text and the significance of turning Bellow's brief novel into the visual form of film. In *Seize the Day*, moving from the written word to the specular text of its cinematic version starring Robin Williams sheds light on the politics of masochism and pain as delineated by Bellow and as espoused by Silverman. Whereas Bellow gives us a character type for the post-World War Two era, Silverman presents a program for individual psychological and collective social change. Released in 1986, three decades after the novel's publication, the film, as Gerhard Bach suggests, puts a visible face on Tommy's problems.[1] However, this attempt by director Fielder Cook and screenwriter Ronald Ribman to visualize Tommy's weakness and limitations suggests difficulties in reconstructing masculinity. Turning *Seize the Day* into a film examines the consequences of visualizing masculinity as a form of male subjectivity in film and theory.

1

Tommy's moral masochism has been analyzed by Daniel Weiss, who transforms the novel into a case history of classic Freudian masochism and neurosis. Weiss writes, "The broadest psychoanalytic category within which Tommy Wilhelm operates is that of the moral masochist, the victim, for whom suffering is a *modus vivendi*, a means of self-justification."[2] Weiss reconstructs Tommy's psyche as a moral masochist.

The ultimate sacrifice of the moral masochist to the love object accounts for his greatest paradox, his perverse refusal to "please" the parent in any rational sense of the word. The masochist identifies himself with the hating love object. He turns against himself, not his own sadism but the sadism of the parent. His guilt becomes the guilt the hating parent should feel if his cruelties are unjust. Since the parent cannot be wrong, the child must then feel guilty for him. He must be the bad child who deserves such chastisement.[3]

In *Male Subjectivity at the Margins*, Silverman incorporates moral masochism into her theory of male subjectivity and marginality that builds on Lacan's transformation of Freud's original paradigm of the individual in culture. In Silverman's theory of masculinity and gender, Freud's dynamic interactive agencies of id, ego, and superego become a Lacanian semiotic and psychoanalytic construction of the self. She emphasizes the relationship of the subjective "I" of nothingness and potentiality to the socially constructed "moi" of the imaginary and fantasy. For Silverman all objects of vision appear to the subject on a screen of cultural and historical context. In addition, Freud emphasizes the determining influence of the "primal scene" of parental sexuality as well as the structuring of sexuality and psychic development through the resolution of the Oedipal and castration complexes. In contrast, for Lacan as Silverman interprets him, more attention needs to be given to the specular basis of sexuality and identity in which the mirror stage and body image initiate the subject's self-reflection as the psychic foundation of all sexuality. The alignment of what Silverman calls the subject's unconscious fantasy of desire with its body ego and self-image helps to form the subject's identity and position within the cultural and ideological order.[4]

Moreover, the concentration in Freud on the psychological implications of biological differences evolves into Silverman's emphasis on the merger of specularity with castration, difference, otherness. Maintaining that subjects are constructed within specularity as well as being determined by biological and psychological forces, Silverman distinguishes between the look and the gaze in cinema, describing the look as a visual statement of desire and absence and the gaze as a kind of transcendent visual moment of self-recognition comparable to the formation of the linguistic ''moi'' or self-image. The interaction between the look and gaze engenders a visual or specular text for the relationship of specularity and subjectivity. In addition, for Silverman specularity structures and signifies the psychic organization of masochism. The relationship of specularity and masochism, which will be discussed later, provides the foundation for gender reconstruction and cultural transformation (Silverman, 1–12).

The focus throughout *Seize the Day* on vision, appearance, spectacle, acting, and self-image suggests the novel's relevance to Silverman's thesis concerning the significance of specularity to the construction of male subjectivity. Indeed, from the very first line of the novel, Bellow establishes the connection between external appearance and Tommy Wilhelm's masochistic interior psyche as mediated by his desire to be an actor – to present a contrived performance of the self to the world: ''When it came to concealing his troubles, Tommy Wilhelm was not less capable than the next fellow. So at least he thought, and there was a certain amount of evidence to back him up. He had once been an actor – no, not quite, an extra – and he knew what acting should be'' (3). This opening line should be taken ironically, as Tommy himself later realizes (14). The psychology behind the statement contradicts its apparent meaning. Tommy yearns to reveal his deepest weaknesses and most intense emotions to all who can see. He dedicates himself to such self-exposure.

For Bellow the tension between appearance and inner feelings raises the issue of the construction of vision. He proposes that our understanding of what we see stems from psychic and cultural structures and predispositions. It concerns a semiotics of facial and physical gesture, as in acting, and it relates to an interior domain of ambivalence that has been occupied by psychoanalysis. Thus, Tommy describes the man at the newsstand in a way that complicates the meaning of vision: "Rubin, the man at the newsstand, had poor eyes. They may not have been actually weak but they were poor in expression, with lacy lids that furled down at the corners. He dressed well. It didn't seem necessary – he was behind the counter most of the time – but he dressed very well" (5). "Poor eyes" problematizes the notion of vision. Bellow allows the idea of bad eyesight to remain by not totally refuting the usual meaning of "poor eyes" as suggesting bad vision. "They may not have been actually weak" keeps the question of eyesight open and emphasizes the psychological and social complexity of vision. The man "behind the counter" dresses "well" but remains partially hidden. Who sees, who cares, Bellow seems to ask.

Bellow immediately compounds the complexity regarding vision by adding a sexual dimension to what and how we see. Rubin comments on Tommy's shirt. " 'That's a real knocked-out shirt you got on,' said Rubin. 'Where's it from, Saks?' " Tommy answers, " 'No, it's a Jack Fagman – Chicago' " (5). This remark instantly impugns the structure and direction of Tommy's sexuality. The shirt and the statement by Tommy function as signs of unconscious ambiguity and incoherence.

After this exchange, Bellow articulates how Tommy sees himself. Besides exhibiting Tommy's insecurity and split psyche, Bellow's style here warrants special attention because of its cinematic quality. He describes a kind of interior camera in Tommy's mind, an internal mirror that anticipates contemporary criticism's fascination with the look and the gaze, specularity and psyche. His self-consciousness compares to the gaze of otherness that goes beyond a singular look.

Even when his spirits were low, Wilhelm could still wrinkle his forehead in a pleasing way. Some of the slow, silent movements of his face were very attractive. He went back a step, as if to stand away from himself and get a better look at his shirt. His glance was comic, a comment upon his untidiness. He liked to wear good clothes, but once he had put it on each article appeared to go its own way. Wilhelm, laughing, panted a little; his teeth were small; his cheeks when he laughed and puffed grew round, and he looked much younger than his years. In the old days when he was a college freshman and wore a raccoon coat and a beanie on his large blond head his father used to say that, big as he was, he could charm a bird out of a tree. Wilhelm had great charm still. (5–6)

The visionary process embedded in Wilhelm's mind in this paragraph dramatizes Silverman's elucidation of the look and gaze in *Male Subjectivity at the Margins*. She also points to the sexual complexity of vision. Silverman writes,

[W]e are all dependent for our identity upon the "clicking" of an imaginary camera. This metaphoric apparatus is what Lacan calls the "gaze." The gaze does not "photo-graph" the subject directly, but only through the mediation of the screen, i.e., through the repertoire of culturally intelligible images. Unfortunately, all such images are ideologically marked in some way; at the very least, they are carriers of sexual and racial difference, but they also project values of class, age, and nationality onto those who are seen through them. (Silverman, 353)

Freud's connection of the body ego to the psychic ego, as Silverman sees it, finds confirmation in how Tommy regards himself. Silverman writes "the ego is for Freud 'first and foremost a bodily ego' – or, as [James] Strachey explains in an authorized gloss, 'derived from bodily sensations, chiefly from those springing from the surface of the body' " (Silverman, 188). In *Seize the Day*, Tommy's bodily ego, his sense of his body and its relation to his identity, opposes his rational awareness of his potential. He sees his body through a psyche of masochistic self-hatred. After Rubin tells him, " 'Well, y'lookin' pretty sharp today' " (6), Tommy greedily grabs at the compliment: "And Wilhelm said gladly, 'Am I? Do you really think so?' " (6).

However, Wilhelm cannot acquiesce to such a favorable view of himself. Looking at "his reflection in the glass cupboard full of cigar boxes, among the grand seals and paper damask and the gold-embossed portraits of famous men" (6), he really sees himself as another object on display like the brand name cigars. "You had to allow for the darkness and deformations of the glass, but he thought he didn't look too good" (6). Of course, he really sees the accumulated images of how he has seen himself in the past, usually as a grotesque animal-type figure such as a hippopotamus (6, 15, 29) or as a "big clunk" (29):

He began to be half amused at the shadow of his own marveling, troubled, desirous eyes, and his nostrils and his lips. Fair-haired hippopotamus! – that was how he looked to himself. He saw a big round face, a wide, flourishing red mouth, stump teeth. And the hat, too; and the cigar, too. I should have done hard labor all my life, he reflected. Hard honest labor that tires you out and makes you sleep. I'd have worked off my energy and felt better. Instead, I had to distinguish myself – yet. (6–7)

Reflecting in his mind on the reflection in the glass, he condemns himself to hard labor for how he looks and what he has done with his appearance. Interestingly, he contextualizes this inner vision of himself in terms of Hollywood images, thereby conflating, as Silverman suggests, both the external social image and interior psychic images: "And if as a young man he had got off to a bad start, it was due to this very same face. Early in the nineteen-thirties, because of his striking looks, he had been very briefly considered star material, and he had gone to Hollywood. There for seven years, stubbornly, he had tried to become a screen artist" (7). We soon learn that this Hollywood opportunity really grew out of a scam, and that even during this episode he was condemned as a failure who loses the girl to real stars. "Why, he thought, he cast me even then for a loser" (21).

2

In the beginning of the novel, Wilky anticipates meeting his father, a successful and wealthy retired doctor, in the dining room of the New York City hotel where they both live in separate quarters. Dreading the encounter but punishing himself further through procrastination, he mentally reenacts his miserable situation. Realizing with masochistic relish that "His father was ashamed of him," Wilky also notes of his father, "how we love looking fine in the eyes of the world – how beautiful are the old when they are doing a snow job!" (13). Wilky's delayed entrance into the dining room to see his father gives spatial and temporal structure to the emotional chaos of the psychological distance between father and son.

No wonder Wilhelm delayed the moment when he would have to go into the dining room. He had moved to the end of Rubin's counter. He had opened the *Tribune*; the fresh pages dropped from his hands; the cigar was smoked out and the hat did not defend him. He was wrong to suppose that he was more capable than the next fellow when it came to concealing his troubles. They were clearly written out upon his face. He wasn't even aware of it." (14)

As the novel dramatizes the struggle in Wilky's mind, Bellow tightly entwines the relationship between his psychic anxiety and his presentation of himself to the world through his name. Significantly, for Wilky naming relates to his acting. Changing his name as an actor involves rebellion against his father whose punishing authority has been internalized within him as a relentless super-ego. Disowning the name of the father breaks the boundaries of the family and proposes maturity and independence. "In California he became Tommy Wilhelm. Dr. Adler would not accept the change. Today he still called his son Wilky, as he had done for more than forty years" (24). Changing his name as part of an acting career literally presumes a new identity within a new environment. Wilky considers acting, name changing, and leaving home precisely this way as an act of manhood. " 'I was too mature for college. I was a big boy, you see. Well, I thought, when do you start to become a man?' " (15). From a psychoanalytical point of view, the name change challenges the whole patriarchal order. The father's name involves the law-of-the-father, a linguistic fulfillment of the threat of castration. The law-of-the-father in the form of the father's name imposes the verbal sign of incorporation in the father's domain of authority. This authority provides the foundation for the meaning of all symbols of identity and authority. As Silverman notes, ''Lacan also equates culture with the Name-of-the-Father.'' Quoting from Lacan's ''The Function and Field of Speech and Language in Psychoanalysis'' in *Ecrits*, Silverman writes: ''It is in the *name of the father* that we must recognize the support of the symbolic function which, from the dawn of history, has identified his person with the figure of the law'' (Silverman, 37). Silverman adds: ''The Name-of-the-Father is also lived by the boy as the paternal legacy which will be his if he renounces the mother, and identifies with the father'' (Silverman, 40). Through this Oedipal process, the individual participates in the symbolic order of patriarchal ideology and power. Thus, by challenging the traditional order of the name-of-the-father, as Silverman suggests, one also subverts what she terms the ''dominant fiction'' (Silverman, 30, 34, 40, 41) of male and patriarchal authority in a way that questions the structure of society and inevitably also the nature of gender and sexuality: ''Our dominant fiction calls upon the male subject to see himself, and the female subject to recognize and desire him, only through the mediation of images of an unimpaired masculinity. It urges both the male and the female subject, that is, to deny all knowledge of male castration by believing in the commensurability of penis and phallus, actual and symbolic father'' (Silverman, 42). Silverman further warns that ''the dominant fiction not only offers the representational system by means of which the subject typically assumes a sexual identity, and takes on the desires commensurate with that identity, but forms the stable core around which a nation's and a period's 'reality' coheres'' (Silverman, 41).

In changing his name, Wilky begins a battle he cannot win, a war in which his own masochism foredooms to defeat. Changing his name merely reenforces his alienation from his father rather than asserting his own identity. Accordingly, Wilky finally goes

78

to find his father in the dining room only after he has completed his own full course of psychic self-abuse by attacking himself, going down the entire menu of failures, guilts, and self-punishments until "he was nearly at the end of his rope." He spots "his father's small head in the sunny bay at the farther end, and heard his precise voice." Wilky then must walk a gauntlet of stares that elicits a visible awareness of his precarious situation. "It was with an odd sort of perilous expression that Wilhelm crossed the dining room" (30).

Silverman's work suggests one possible insight into Wilky's "odd sort of perilous expression." The "perilous expression" transfers Tommy's psychic dismemberment to the look on his face, enacting an important principle in Silverman's Lacanian conception of castration. Using Lacan's shift in the definition of castration, Silverman emphasizes castration as a visual phenomenon. As Silverman says, Lacan's theory "repeatedly locates lack at the level of the eye, defining castration as the alterity of the gaze" (Silverman, 155). Tommy's expression as he crosses the dining room to his father makes a spectacle of his complicity in his impairment. It is in part a self-inflicted wound performed through the visualization of dismemberment. The expression re-enforces the significance of symbolic castration in the novel. Thus, the refusal of Tommy's wife to allow him to keep his beloved dog "Scissors" (110), and the warnings of his surrogate father, Dr. Tamkin, about enjoying guilt all relate to Tommy's castration complex. Talking of Tommy's wife, Tamkin, a wonderful mixture of the comic and venal, says: "Why do you let her make you suffer so? It defeats the original object in leaving her. Don't play her game. Now, Wilhelm, I'm trying to do you some good. I want to tell you, don't marry suffering. Some people do. They get married to it, and sleep and eat together, just as husband and wife. If they go with joy they think it's adultery" (98).

Tommy's walk through the dining room fulfills the association, from the beginning of the novel, of castration and external appearance, the connection between acting and the presentation to the world of a visible sign of the absence of manhood. Significantly, whereas Tommy saw acting as an attempt to achieve manhood, the novel repeatedly indicates that others' perception of him and perhaps even his own unconscious self-image really proffer homosexuality as his form of masculinity. Thus, we recall the peculiar reference by Tommy to his "Fagman" shirt. This epithet as a kind of badge of identity achieves greater significance in light of a later exchange between father and son. The father insinuates that perhaps Tommy was forced to leave a job because of a possible homosexual incident. Noting his son's obsession with his failures and perhaps intuiting an unconscious tension, the father says: " 'Since you have to talk and can't let it alone, tell the truth. Was there a scandal – a woman?' " After "Wilhelm fiercely defended himself. 'No, Dad, there wasn't any woman. I told you how it was,' " Bellow writes, " 'Maybe it was a man, then,' the old man said wickedly" (51). The vigor of Tommy's immediate protest reveals an element of overcompensation: "Shocked, Wilhelm stared at him with burning pallor and dry lips. His skin looked a little yellow. 'I don't think you know what you're talking about,' he answered after a moment. 'You shouldn't let your imagination run so free. Since you've been living here on Broadway you must think you understand life, up to date. You ought to know your own son a little better. Let's drop that, now' " (51–2).

Moreover, homosexuality associates Tommy with a particular form of homosexuality of great interest to Silverman. Her study of marginalized male subjectivity relates homosexuality to moral masochism, the feminine, and the visualization of castration. Silverman argues that although Freud distinguishes between three forms of masochism – erotogenic or pleasure in pain, feminine, and moral – such distinctions immediately collapse. "However, no sooner are these distinctions enumerated than they begin to erode" (Silverman, 188). She argues that moral masochism and the feminine evolve into "homosexuality-as-feminine-corporeality" (Silverman, 348). Masochism and the feminine structure homosexuality as an alternative form of male subjectivity. "Implicit, then, in the notion of masochism, whether feminine or moral, would seem to be the experience of corporeal pleasure, or – to be more precise – corporeal pleasure-in-pain" (Silverman, 188).

Tommy exemplifies the character type Silverman describes.

Even to some in the novel, he exists at some level of his psyche as a woman in the body of a man who wishes to be loved by the father rather than to identify with him. Indeed, Tommy's perennial groveling before his father for love and sympathy – "He was well aware that he didn't stand a chance of getting sympathy from his father, who said he kept his for real ailments" (43) – relates to his unconscious conflicted identification with his mother and guilt over mixed and ambiguous feelings about her death. Thus, Tommy reminds his father about his mother's death with a sense of guilt he would like to share with him: " 'Wasn't it the year Mother died? What year was that?' He asked the question with an innocent frown on his Golden Grimes, dark blond face. *What year was it!* As though he didn't know the year, the month, the day, the very hour of his mother's death" (27).

Put another way, Tommy's mental state compares to what Silverman terms as "this convergence of desire for the father and identification with his penetration of the mother" (Silverman, 173), a relationship analogous to Freud's classic case study of the Wolf Man whose neurosis derived from his "unconscious sexuality" (Silverman, 165) regarding his father. In trying to establish and then reinvent his identity as an actor, Tommy appears caught, as Silverman says, in "the possibility of assuming a subject-position at the intersection of the positive and the negative Oedipus complexes" (Silverman, 173). Trapped in the Oedipal dilemma between a positive relationship to his father that prohibits and represses the desire for the mother and a negative relationship that makes the father the object of desire so as to avoid the Oedipal attraction to the mother, Tommy founders in a regressive and nearly infantile state that manifests itself in unclean and neurotic gestures. Thus, the doctor feels revulsion over what he sees as Wilky's "filth." "What a Wilky he had given to the world! Why, he didn't even wash his hands in the morning. . . . Wilhelm lived in worse filth than a savage" (36–7). Wilky's incessant gestures are equally intolerable: "But Dr. Adler was thinking, Why the devil can't he stand still when we're talking? He's either hoisting his pants up and down by the pockets or jittering with his feet. A regular mountain of tics, he's getting to be" (28–9). Also, the chaos of Tommy's sexual orientation and identification finds further confirmation in the way the book radically changes point-of-view and alters the subjective position and voice of the main characters. The book continually moves between Tommy's and his father's perspectives so that at the end of the novel, Tommy desperately strives to assert his subjective identity: "*I labor, I spend, I strive, I design, I love, I cling, I uphold, I give way, I envy, I long, I scorn, I die, I hide, I want*" (115).

Bellow brilliantly brings together all these highly complex and diverse elements of psychology, sexuality, and vision in a marvelously concrete and deceptively simple encounter between father and son that becomes the emotional and thematic climax of the novel. Tommy once again seeks out his father after he has lost all his money in commodity market dealings engineered by the enigmatic Dr. Tamkin. Significantly, Tommy finds him in the massage room, a place of naked male bodies that emphasizes the key issue of sexuality, gender, and vision. "On the tables naked men were lying" (107). The scene focuses on a man Tommy sees, "an athlete, strikingly muscled, powerful and young, with a strong white curve to his genital and a half-angry smile on his mouth" (107–8). The "half-angry smile" and "genital" illustrate Silverman's fusion of the feminine and the masochist in the homosexual. Comparing in this "sexual territorialization of the body," "the male mouth with the female genitals," Silverman argues that in this model "the homosexual subject does not so much flee from the mother as relocate her within himself" (Silverman, 358, 10, 372), a phrase that aptly describes Tommy and his latent attraction to the naked man.

Wilky's appearance before his father in the massage room dramatizes his sexually ambiguous relationship to him. At the level of spectacle, Tommy appears unnatural and abnormal to his father. "Dr. Adler opened his eyes into Wilhelm's face" (108). The thrust of the sentence accentuates hostility and fear. "At once he saw the trouble in it, and by an instantaneous reflex he removed himself from the danger of contagion, and he said serenely, 'Well, have you taken my advice, Wilky?' " referring to his recommendation " 'To take a swim and get a massage.' " When Wilky appeals once again for help, the father reacts with horror. Wilky says to his father " 'But one word from you, just a word, would go a long way. I've never asked you for very much. But you are not a kind man. You don't give the little bit I beg you for' '' (109–10). The doctor responds viciously. In contrast to his son's masochism, he will not allow another person, not even his son, to become his cross. '' 'You want to make yourself into my cross. But I am not going to pick up a cross. I'll see you dead, Wilky, by Christ, before I let you do that to me' '' (110).

The father's next response to Wilky's whine summarizes the emotional and psychological center of the novel: '' 'Go away from me now. It's torture for me to look at you, you slob!' cried Dr. Adler'' (110). The torture of the doctor's look upon his son matches his own fear of castration and women with his son's embodiment, in both their eyes, of deficiency and inadequacy. The combination of horror and guilt in the doctor's look relates directly to his ambivalence regarding the mother as part of his general disavowal of difference and weakness. In addition, Wilky's obsession with being normal reenforces the perception of his father and others about Wilky's sexuality (51, 53, 73). He tells the doctor, '' 'More than half of my life is over. More than half. And now you tell me I'm not even normal' '' (54).

Wilky's condition of emasculation and his personification of the system of visual castration and masochism in combination with the feminine and the homosexual recalls Silverman's insistence that the "dominant fiction" of masculinity by definition denies and disavows castration and weakness. As already noted, she argues that the patriarchal order maintains a fiction of "unimpaired masculinity." She maintains that "traditional masculinity is predicated" on the denial of "lack, specularity, and alterity" and that women are expected to reenforce this disavowal (Silverman, 50–1). In radical contrast with this organization of power, she hopes "to show that male mastery rests upon an abyss" that must be recognized so that "every subject's encounter with the death drive might become in time more of an everyday occurrence – that the typical male subject, like his female counterpart, might learn to live with lack" (Silverman, 65). Calling for a new '' 'libidinal politics' '' that exposes "the murderous logic of traditional male subjectivity," Silverman aligns "marginal male subjectivities" with '' 'the feminine' '' to subvert "the line of paternal succession." The male subject that she envisions will accede "to his castration, his specularity, and the profound 'otherness' of his 'self,' " thereby "embracing desires and identifications which are in excess of the positive Oedipus complex." Say " 'no' to power" she says, as though offering a campaign slogan for gender reconstruction (Silverman, 389, 388, 389).

To some extent, Bellow's position on masculinity coincides with Silverman's program of reconstructing gender to counter the power of unitary masculinity. In *Dangling Man*, Bellow exhibits impatience with an attitude of unrestrained masculine power and aggression. In this novel, Bellow also anticipates the concern in *Seize the Day* for the relationship of external signs of behavior to inner being and character.

> For this is an era of hardboiled-dom. Today, the code of the athlete, of the tough boy – an American inheritance, I believe, from the English gentleman – that curious mixture of striving, asceticism, and rigor, the origins of which some trace back to Alexander the Great – is stronger than ever. Do you have feelings? There are correct and incorrect ways of indicating them. Do you have an inner life? It is nobody's business but your own. Do you have emotions? Strangle them. To a degree, everyone obeys this code.[5]

This view of masculinity mocks the dominance during this historical period of the Great Depression and the Second World War of a Hemingway version of masculinity that pervaded not only Hollywood but our entire culture as well. In the twelve years that separated *Dangling Man* from *Seize the Day*, much changed in regard to the values and ideals of masculinity. Wilky clearly embodies the opposite extreme of "hardboiled-dom." His desperate search for both love and punishment through the continual exposure of his inner feelings clearly anticipates the way the internal has been unleashed with a vengeance in contemporary culture. No longer strangled, internal feelings demand instant expression and gratification in today's culture. Bellow's portrayal of Wilky demonstrates the need for some inhibition of this drive toward public exposure of inner selves and inchoate needs. He seems to be castigating what has become a character type in our times and what he himself termed in another novel, "the victim.'' Ironically, Bellow's presentation of Wilky's manhood may set him at odds with Silverman's program of male subjectivity, while enlisting Tommy Wilhelm in her cause.

Discussing a wide range of directors and authors from Frank Capra and Rainer Werner Fassbinder to T. E. Lawrence, Henry James, and Marcel Proust, Silverman articulates a program of alternative masculinities and gender relationships that challenge the power of unitary masculinity. In contrast to this program, Wilky never directly confronts his symbolic castration, deals with his impulse toward death, or recognizes the feminine in himself; he only represents the consequences of these forces at the unconscious level. Nevertheless, in his passionate embrace of masochistic punishment, denial, and emasculation, Tommy typifies in some ways Silverman's position of proffering alternatives to traditional masculine power.

3

In *Seize the Day*, Bellow brilliantly conveys Tommy's emasculation through a complex dynamic of interior monologue, fluid point of view, unconventional use of narrative and time. Although Tommy's rejection of power and his accommodation to lack seem to exemplify some of Silverman's proposals for forming new paradigms of male subjectivity, his total immersion in weakness leaves him thoroughly isolated and without any conceivable prospects for change. Because all his experiences become internalized in the form of masochistic self-abuse, he lives without the alliances that would enable him to construct a promising future. His attempts to ''seize the day'' devour experience and incorporate others within his psyche in a way that separates him from reality.

Tommy's position of absolute isolation creates a serious problem for the film version of the novel as to how to visually construct his place in society when the world of his mind encompasses his real living environment. The difficulty in a film of visually mapping out a social world without clear boundaries between inner and outer space requires a solution that an audience can visually recognize. Thus, in trying to put a face on

Wilky's masochism, Robin Williams makes him merely a victim undergoing a nervous breakdown, a good guy forever down on his luck. As interpreted by Williams, Tommy's incapacity to respond effectively to his condition stems directly from the powerful forces arrayed against him – his father, his passive mother, an unsympathetic wife, an unfair boss, a devoted but inadequate lover, disloyal friends who won't help, including one played by Tony Roberts in a particularly pathetic business lunch scene in which Wilky picks up the tab out of false pride. Throughout the film, he refuses to defend himself against his wife's spiteful attacks, resisting his girlfriend's admonishments to be more aggressive, and he continues generous child support because of his affection for his children.

Williams's portayal of Tommy as a thorough victim draws attention to the difficulties involved in visually articulating moral masochism and making marginalized male subjectivity an effective instrument for change. Instead of developing Tommy into a hero of absence and lack, Williams makes him an object of pity to win over the audience's support. By widening Tommy's internal war to include all that surrounds him, Williams's whining probably invites a sadistic response from some in his audience to equal Tommy's masochism.

Nevertheless, the intensity, depth, and range of Silverman's seminal theory demonstrate the potential for studying the complexity of male characters in films and literature. In fact, several recent studies consider representations of diverse masculinities in a broad range of important actors, including Silverman's own original analysis of Jimmy Stewart in Capra's *It's a Wonderful Life* and Fredric March and Dana Andrews in William Wyler's *The Best Years of Our Lives*. Other significant works include Dennis Bingham's study of "masculinities in the films" of Stewart, Jack Nicholson, and Clint Eastwood in *Acting Male*, and Graham McCann's portrayals of Montgomery Clift, Marlon Brando, and James Dean in *Rebel Males*. Also, James Naremore's work, *Acting in the Cinema*, includes indispensable interpretations of Stewart, Brando, Robert De Niro, and Cary Grant, among others.[6] All these works expatiate on the varieties of male subjectivities presented by these actors. They attest to the pervasive presence in the performances of these actors of themes of importance to marginalized male subjectivity: castration, difference, specularity, otherness, the fragility of patriarchal positions, bisexuality. In innumerable films, these actors have complicated the representation of masculinity. From Clift in *From Here to Eternity* and *A Place in the Sun*, Brando in *On the Waterfront*, and Stewart in *It's a Wonderful Life* to more contemporary actors such as Al Pacino, Dustin Hoffman, Robert Redford, and most recently and remarkably, Clint Eastwood, all modify classic unitary masculinism to convey complexity, ambivalence, and a degree of bisexuality through speech patterns, physical positioning, and body language.

To some, Robin Williams belongs in this pantheon of actors of intelligence and sensitivity who dare to experiment with performances of alternative male identifications and subjectivities. For example, Lizzie Francke in a recent article, ''Being Robin'' in *Sight and Sound*, the journal of the British Film Institute, argues that since the inception of his career, Williams's acting persona ''could be considered a symptom of the changes of the 70s, as feminism began to question notions of masculinity and femininity and the old models of maleness were revealed to be far from satisfactory.''[7] Accordingly, Williams seems like a logical choice to play Tommy Wilhelm.

Unfortunately, the strategy of the film and Williams's performance rely excessively on turning the inward spiral of Tommy's interior chaos into all kinds of maddening horizontal movements: driving insanely in his car to escape unseen forces; walking and running hysterically through the streets of New York to discover new ways of losing his money or himself; wandering abstractly through his New York hotel in search of the elusive father figure locked tightly in some secret corner of his mind. Given the complex relationship of Tommy's masochism to gender, the feminine, and the homosexual, the challenge of the movie involves visualizing his psychic condition of castration. It must visually articulate this condition through performance and the other elements of film, including editing and mise-en-scène, without deteriorating into Williams's aggressive histrionics. It needs to place castration within the scopic regime itself to allow the film to exploit cinema's inherent specular text of the look and gaze that locates, again in Silverman's phrase, "lack at the level of the eye, defining castration as the alterity of the gaze" (Silverman, 155). As she develops the relationship of the look and gaze to film, the "look" like language itself works to distinguish being from social definition and determination. "One of the crucial features of Lacan's redefinition of castration," she says, "has been to shift it away from this obligatory anatomical referent to the void installed by language" (Silverman, 154–5). Like language, the look by organizing vision contests the existential unknown of human identity and emphasizes the intrinsic division of the human psyche. "The implicit starting point for virtually every formulation this book will propose is the assumption that lack of being is the irreducible condition of subjectivity," Silverman writes. "In acceding to language, the subject forfeits all existential reality, and foregoes [sic] any future possibility of 'wholeness' " (Silverman, 4).

The look as a kind of abyss on which the individual constructs subjectivity and dramatizes "lack at the level of the eye" can be found in many classic Hollywood films: on Montgomery Clift's face as he stands alone at a party at the Eastman mansion in *A Place in the Sun* or as he watches Donna Reed walk off with another soldier in *From Here to Eternity*; in Brando's scene with Rod Steiger in *On the Waterfront* when he admits to being a "bum" rather than a "contender"; in the stolid expression on Gary Cooper's face as he walks out of a saloon in *High Noon* and into the realization on the abandoned street that he stands absolutely alone in the town he has repeatedly saved from crime and desolation. The great moments in classic films often position the male characters alone in a confrontation with themselves and with their loss and inadequacy.

In contrast to such moments, Robin Williams in *Seize the Day* fills every scene with something substantial and palpable that essentializes his state of mind and his identity. Existential tension shrivels to self-pity. From the opening scene of Wilky's frantic driving, honking, and addictive smoking to the finale of hysterical weeping at a stranger's funeral, the screen spills over with the tears of his victimization. Thus, in the film's beginning, he greets road construction that delays his drive to nowhere with a whine, "Now what." Similarly, the early flashbacks revisit his history of mistreatment by others.

The film's inability to engage the novel's linkage of masochism, castration, the body, and the feminization of homosexuality reveals itself in one early flashback that introduces Olive, his Catholic girlfriend. Before presenting Olive, the film mechanically shows Wilky's hysterical tirade against his boss who has given Wilky's "territory" to a son-in-law. "What does he got that I don't have," Wilky screams before smashing his fist and arm through a glass window. The bandaged wound appears as a potential sign of both physical and psychological dismemberment in the next cut with Olive as Tommy describes the incident to her, wildly bragging about the impression his display made on the other workers. His exaggerated expressiveness marks a form of verbal and physical overcompensation for his failure. As he talks, they both undress, intimating the sexual as well as the psychological dimensions of the self-inflicted wound. His frustrated and uncoordinated movements force him to struggle to remove his shirt. The shyness and fragility of Olive make the scene interesting, promising the potential exposure of weakness and ambivalence. Her drawn face and her thin body suggest a kind of spiritual anemia. She moves from the bed where she has lowered her stockings to a screen behind which she peers at Wilky as she undresses while he continues his tirade. The protection of the screen implies sexual difference and inhibition. However, the visual display of uncertainty becomes overwhelmed by his verbal bombast and wild gestures, her pleas for resolution to their situation, and the heavy-handed intention of Williams and director Fielder Cook to invest as much pathos in the scene as possible. Words smother the visual articulation of difference. Similarly, in a brilliant structural analysis of how "place, space, pace" change in moving from the novel to the film, Michael Shiels says the scene places Tommy "in what can only be viewed as an uneasily visualized relationship to his background."[8]

Moreover, rather than embracing the body in all its ambiguity, vulnerability, and difference, the film of *Seize the Day* turns the body into the enemy, thereby epitomizing what an array of film theorists and directors, according to James Naremore, considers to be an inherent element in the aesthetic form of all film, namely its visible demonstration of death and biology. Naremore claims that Jean-Luc Godard summarizes the views of many other notables of film, including Jean Cocteau and Andre Bazin: " 'The person one films is growing older and will die. We film, therefore, a moment when death is working.' "⁹ This symbiosis of death and cinema becomes an obsession with *Seize the Day* to the point of making the fear of death a crucial force in the film. The film of *Seize the Day* hates Dr. Adler not because he is a self-obsessed, self-centered, and selfish old man who psychologically violates his son as an unforgiving, uncompromising, and unrelenting moralistic super-ego, but because he is old and his friends are old and they all look old. From the moment the film enters the doctor's world at the Hotel Gloriana, we are in an uptown New York Auschwitz of the aging and the abandoned. Here the elderly, even when bound for glory, are by definition grotesque and horrific. Castration, sexual difference, and ambivalence have been personified and cast as elderly New York Jews who typify the cultural hatred of the body and biology. The aging body becomes a Jewish body, merging fears of death with fears of difference and otherness. Distorted lighting and restricted physical movements transmogrify the Gloriana residents into creeping aliens and revolting freaks with grotesque physical features, gestures, and expressions. The worst have physical deformities or own miserable, uncontrollable pets without adequate house-training, perhaps emulating the difficulties of their aging owners. Even the relatively younger residents who are retired, such as Dr. Tamkin/Jerry Stiller and his cardplaying cronies, are depicted as weird New York oddities.

As played with painful precision by the brilliant character actor Joseph Wiseman, Dr. Adler comes off as death incarnate, especially in the massage room scene. After a high angle shot reveals the fragility of Dr. Adler's thin body on the massage table, the camera shoots him in straight-on medium close-ups, keeping his head and body horizontal to the table, the embodiment of a ghostly death-in-life. Thus, without confronting any of the confusing complexity of castration, sexual ambivalence, parental authority, maturation, and identification, Wilky in the film finally has an enemy to share with everyone, his father as the personification of the grim reaper. In facing death in the figure of his father, Wilky represents the victimization of all people facing death. The whining, crying, pleading, frowning, cringing portrayal of manhood by Robin Williams institutionalizes victimization. The film's avoidance of symbolic castration and loss at the level of the look, meaning as an inexorable aspect of all human experience and all gender construction, male or female, trivializes the crisis of manhood and male subjectivity articulated by Bellow and Silverman. It therefore also avoids Silverman's challenge to live on the "abyss" with lack and loss, but it confirms Bellow's view of Wilky's manhood. Tommy becomes a victim for all seasons, unfortunately several decades too early to make it on afternoon talk shows as a perfect character type for our times. Poor Tommy, always the unhappy loser.

NOTES

1   See Gerhard P. Bach, " 'Howling like a Wolf from the City Window': The Cinematic Realization of *Seize the Day*," *Saul Bellow Journal* 7 (1988): 71–83.

2   Daniel Weiss, "Caliban on Prospero: A Psychoanalytic Study of the Novel *Seize the Day*, by Saul Bellow" in Irving Malin, ed., *Psychoanalysis and American Fiction* (New York: Dutton, 1965), p. 287.

3   Ibid., pp. 291–2.

4   See Kaja Silverman, *Male Subjectivity at the Margins* (New York: Routledge, 1992), pp. 1–12. All subsequent references to this book will be to this edition and will be included parenthetically in the text.

5   Bellow, *Dangling Man* (New York: Avon, 1944), p. 7.

6   See Dennis Bingham, *Acting Male: Masculinities in the Films of James Stewart, Jack Nicholson, and Clint Eastwood* (New York: Rutgers University Press, 1994); Graham McCann, *Rebel Males: Clift, Brando, and Dean* (New York: Rutgers University Press, 1993); James Naremore, *Acting in the Cinema* (Berkeley: University of California Press, 1988).

7   Lizzie Francke, "Being Robin," *Sight and Sound* 4 (April 1994): 28.

8   Michael Shiels, "Place, Space, and Pace: A Cinematic Reading of *Seize*

the Day'' in Gerhard P. Bach, ed., *Saul Bellow at Seventy-Five: A Collection of Critical Essays* (Tubingen: Gunter Narr Verlag, 1991), pp. 59, 55.

9 Naremore, *Acting in the Cinema*, p. 20.

5

Yizkor for Six Million:
Mourning the Death of Civilization
in Saul Bellow's *Seize the Day*

EMILY MILLER BUDICK

THERE ARE probably few more assimilated Jewish characters in American literature than Tommy Wilhelm in Saul
Bellow's *Seize the Day*. Nor, for that matter, are there many more
non-Jewish Jewish texts than *Seize the Day*. *Seize the Day* seems to
be about nothing so much as the archetypical struggle between
father and son, whether enacted in Freudian or other, classical
or psychological, terms. No wonder so much criticism on this
novella has (like the preceding essay in this volume by Sam Girgus) moved either in the direction of analyzing the book in terms
of an Oedipal conflict in its two dangerous and mutually destruc-
tive directions, or of detecting other psychological neuroses, specifically in Wilhelm, but in Drs. Adler and Tamkin as well.[1] In
such readings of the novella, either Judaism has no role to play
in the story's thematic and imagistic structure, or it becomes itself
the father (either as divine Father or as patriarchal religion)
against which Wilhelm or Bellow or both struggle to free themselves.

Yet as Michael Kramer points out in the introduction to this
volume, critics of Bellow (many of them Jewish themselves)
have been hesitant to let go so easily the Jewish character of this
text. Indeed, so strong is the desire to find specifically Jewish
meanings in *Seize the Day* that one critic bases an entire interpretation on a telling misreading: that its action takes place on the
holiest of Jewish holidays, the Day of Atonement, Yom Kippur.
Under similar pressure, another critic misreads a crucial line to
claim that the events occur on the *eve* of Yom Kippur, even
though the text clearly indicates that this is not *erev* Yom Kippur.[2] If there is an idea of atonement in this novella, the moment

for such repentance, I suggest, is decidedly yet to come. Furthermore, the narrative implies that such a moment would lead, not toward Jewish renewal (as some critics believe), but away from Judaism altogether. Something besides a stranger is being buried in the funeral scene that concludes the novel, and it is not, as some have assumed, merely a phase of human suffering, either Tommy Wilhelm's personal suffering or the suffering of his people. Rather, the novel is laying to rest Judaism itself – a feature of the text brought into focus by a detail of textual revision: that, as the editor of this volume has noted, the Star of David, which initially marked the funeral as Jewish, loses the specificity of its form in subsequent reprintings of the novella.

Seize the Day does indeed have something to do with Judaism and Jews, and not only because most of its characters (Tommy, Adler, Tamkin, Perls, Rappoport) are nominally Jewish. At the center of the text's dark and despairing consciousness of life in the modern world is a specifically Jewish event. This event remains largely marginal to the text, almost squeezed out of consciousness in its minimalization. Yet it determines almost everything about the novella, from its imagery to its plot to the strangely Jewish/non-Jewish funeral at its conclusion. The event I have in mind is the Nazi Holocaust.

Like other Jewish American writers, Bellow almost never deals directly with the events of the Holocaust. "The Holocaust," Bellow says in a 1990 interview, is one of those things that I haven't been able to "incorporate," "that got away from me."[3] Nonetheless, and also paralleling the situations of other contemporary American Jewish authors, a Holocaust consciousness permeates much of his fiction, especially in the period during and immediately following the war.[4] The major attempts at American Jewish Holocaust writing, excluding some of the more popular fiction of writers like Herman Wouk and Leon Uris, and excluding as well the testimonies of non-American survivors, like Primo Levi, Elie Wiesel, and Jerzy Kosinski, are Susan Schaeffer's *Anya* and Leslie Epstein's *King of the Jews*. A larger and more successful category of American Jewish Holocaust writing, which deals primarily with the consequences of the Holocaust for its survivors and their descendants (though some of these works also include flashbacks to the events of the Holocaust itself) and most of which appear after 1960, includes Philip Roth's "Eli the Fanatic," Edward Wallant's *The Pawnbroker*, Bellow's *Mr. Sammler's Planet*, Cynthia Ozick's *Cannibal Galaxy*, *The Messiah of Stockholm*, and *The Shawl*, some of Rebecca Goldstein's short stories and her recent novel *Mazel*, and a few other works.

By far the largest group of writings, however, like Bellow's *Seize the Day*, touches the event of the Holocaust only tangentially, or in the context of, or for the purposes of, some other textual undertaking. This group contains such stories and novels as Bellow's *The Victim*, Philip Roth's "Defender of the Faith" and the Zuckerman novels, including *The Counterlife*, some of Bernard Malamud's short stories, Cynthia Ozick's "Pagan Rabbi," a few Grace Paley stories, and Rebecca Goldstein's *Mind-Body Problem* and *Late Summer Passion of a Woman of Mind*. To survivors and nonsurvivors alike, the Holocaust has always seemed to be beyond our ability to know, and, therefore, to represent.[5] Writing about the Holocaust, whether historically, philosophically, or theologically, as literary fiction or eye-witness testimony, or trying to convey it through some nonverbal or extra-verbal medium, such as painting or music or video recording, has seemed, again and again, not simply to miss it but to violate it: to distort or trivialize or even to deny it.

A respectful silence would seem the only legitimate response. But it is difficult to imagine what a respectful silence would sound like, and how it would avoid simply obliterating the Holocaust not only from the written historical record but from consciousness itself. Therefore, in many works of American fiction, the inscription of the Holocaust is almost silent, amounting to no more than a word or an allusion. Yet in the works in which such silent inscriptions occur, the stories' ostensible themes – having to do with psychology, philosophy, theology, and love – resound loudly with post-Holocaust messages. In other words, the texts talk about the Holocaust in the only way that seems decorous to some writers: in not talking about it. This is the case as well for literary critics like Lionel Trilling, whose writings constitute a much more sustained engagement with Jewish history than the critical tradition has heretofore imagined.[6]

There are powerful reasons for taking *Seize the Day* as being about the Holocaust in this oblique, understated way. In the first place, the protagonist's adult life virtually spans the period of the war. Tommy first goes to Hollywood in the nineteen thirties, before the major annihilation had begun, and the present moment of the text begins after the revelations of the war, in the early '50s. What has occurred to the Jewish people during these years of Tommy's personal crises is directly introduced into the story by the presence of the German refugee Mr. Perls. Not accidentally, it is Perls who initiates Tommy's philosophizing in the following passage. This passage solidifies the book's otherwise diffuse and oblique allusions to the Holocaust. It also declares the Holocaust the major event, not only of recent Jewish history, but of world history as well:

That sick Mr Perls at breakfast had said that there was no easy way to tell the sane from the mad, and he was right about that in any big city and especially in New York – the end of the world, with its complexity and machinery, bricks and tubes, wires and stones, holes and heights. And was everybody crazy here? What sort of people did you see? Every other man spoke a language entirely his own, which he had figured out by private thinking; he has his own ideas and peculiar ways. If you wanted to talk about a glass of water, you had to start back with God creating the heavens and earth; the apple; Abraham; Moses and Jesus; Rome; the Middle Ages; gunpowder; the Revolution; back to Newton; up to Einstein; then war and Lenin and Hitler. After reviewing this and getting it all straight again you could proceed to talk about a glass of water. "I'm fainting, please get me a little water." You were lucky even then to make yourself understood. And this happened over and over and over with everyone you met. You had to translate and translate, explain and explain, back and forth, and it was the punishment of hell itself not to understand or be understood, not to know the crazy from the sane, the wise from the fools, the young from the old or the sick from the well. The fathers were no fathers and the sons no sons. You had to talk with yourself in the daytime and reason with yourself at night. Who else was there to talk to in a city like New York? (83–4)

From Creation to Hitler. *Seize the Day* is nothing less than counter-scripture. It is Bellow's new post-Holocaust testament, replacing both Old and New Testaments.[7] *Seize the Day* constitutes

Bellow's *yizkor* for the six million, as he mourns for them and for the death of civilization, which their deaths effectively realized. And in this post-Holocaust burial of the Western theological tradition, Judaism itself, as the Old Testament echoes begin to alert us, is not exempt. Therefore, in the funeral scene which ends the book, Bellow's story says *kaddish* not only for the world's lost Jews but for the father of Christian culture, Judaism itself.

On the way to his *kaddish* for Judaism, Bellow provides the full measure of his contempt for European, and even American, culture. For all its insistence on being an American story, set in the most quintessentially American of cities, *Seize the Day* unfolds as something of an allegory of prewar Europe, and, perhaps, postwar Europe as well. Hence the story's setting in the Hotel Gloriana, with its French drapes (4), its "glass cupboard full of cigar boxes, among the grand seals and paper damask and the gold-embossed portraits of famous men" (6) and its "dining-room, which was under Austro-Hungarian management [and] run like a European establishment" (30). That the ironically named Gloriana is a home for old folks may reflect the past-ness of Europe's glory. It may also signify the decrepitude in which this glory existed even before the war. Ironically, this state of decadence and corruption in no way excludes European Jewry. Tommy Wilhelm's (Wilhelm Adler's) name stands for this German-Jewish connection, through no less than an evocation of the Kaiser himself. Bellow deliberately places his story against a backdrop of the very place which had witnessed, only a decade before, the slaughter of European Jewry; and then he plays out his allegory of the European catastrophe with a Jewish cast of characters in the role of European aristocracy.

As in so much of Bellow's fiction, the characters in *Seize the Day* are not only Jewish, but also highly assimilated into Western culture. Nor is this assimilation a feature of the present generation only. Tommy's "mother had belonged to the Reform congregation. His father had no religion" (86). Whatever Tommy Wilhelm's rebellion represents, it does not signal a direct revolt against Judaism. Wilhelm, who, we are told, does not go to synagogue (86), is little troubled by his having a Roman Catholic girlfriend, though she herself dissolves into tears when, on his account, she is late for mass on Sunday morning (94). Similarly, when Wilhelm finally makes his appeal to his father to lend him money, Dr. Adler bursts back at him, "You want to make yourself into my cross. But I am not going to pick up a cross. I'll see you dead, Wilky, by Christ, before I let you do that to me" (110). Whether Dr. Adler is European or American born (it is not clear to me which), he is closely associated with non-American Jewish experience, non-American Jewish assimilation. Even though Dr. Adler claims to "uphold tradition" while his son opts "for the new" (14), the tradition Dr. Adler upholds is obviously not Judaism, and whatever defines the conflict between these generations of Jews, it has nothing to do with an already extinguished commitment to things Jewish.

Bellow's subject, then (in part, at least) may well be Jewish assimilation, which Bellow in some way blames for the destruction of European Jewry. The uncertainties concerning Yom Kippur and the minimalism of the Jewish dimensions in the final funeral scene would seem to support this possibility. So would Dr. Tamkin's lengthy discourse on the real and the pretender soul, which puts forward the popular American idea of a self in disrelation to any historical and social definition which would limit and determine it. Tamkin, crazy man, fraud, speculator, and poet-philosopher, presents a version of Emerson, popularized and largely misunderstood, as the exact antithesis, or so it would appear, of what Dr. Adler means by "tradition," if we understand tradition (within the context of the Hotel Gloriana) to be Adler's roots in old-world culture, either Jewishly or Germanly accented. By invoking Emersonianism in this context, the novella warns that America is by no means immune to the paganism and barbarism that had so recently nearly destroyed European civilization. It raises the question as to whether American individualism is an antidote to catastrophe.

"In here, the human bosom," Tamkin explains to Tommy, "mine, yours, everybody's – there isn't just one soul. There's a lot of souls. But there are two main ones, the real soul and a pretender soul":

Now! Every man realizes that he has to love something or somebody. He feels that he must go outward. "If thou canst not love, what are thou?" . . . Nothing. That's the answer. Nothing. In the heart of hearts – Nothing! So of course you can't stand that and want to be Something, and you try. But instead of being this Something, the man puts it over on everybody instead. You can't be that strict to yourself. You love a *little*. Like you have a dog . . . or give some money to a charity drive. Now that isn't love, is it? What is it? Egotism, pure and simple. It's a way to love the pretender soul. Vanity. Only vanity, is what it is. And social control. The interest of the pretender soul is the same as the interest of the social life, the society mechanism. This is the main tragedy of human life. Oh, it is terrible! Terrible! You are not free. Your own betrayer is inside of you and sells you out. You have to obey him like a slave. He makes you work like a horse. And for what? For who? . . . The true soul is the one that pays the price. It suffers and gets sick, and it realizes that the pretender can't be loved. (70–1)

Through its concern with the authentic soul and with the self-enslavement to society, which sacrifices this soul, Bellow's text recalls passages in both Emerson and Thoreau.[8] This would seem to move, in the name of a quintessential Americanism, in the direction of retrieving some authentic self, a real soul. In Tommy's case, as Tommy himself realizes, this might actually be his buried Jewish self. Bellow coyly invites us to read behind Tamkin's philosophy the possibility of a Jewish recovery. "In Tommy," Wilhelm explains of himself, "he saw the pretender. And even Wilky might not be himself. Might the name of his true soul be the one by which his old grandfather had called him – Velvel?" (72).

This idea is strengthened by an earlier, even more Jewishly (biblically) informed passage, which this passage recalls. This earlier passage concerns Wilhelm's adoption of his stage name, Tommy Wilhelm, which figures his break both from his father and from tradition:

When he was drunk he reproached himself horribly as Wilky. . . . He thought that it was a good thing perhaps that he had not become a success as Tommy since that would not have been a genuine success. Wilhelm would have feared that not he but Tommy had brought it off, cheating Wilky of his birthright. Yes, it had been a stupid thing to do, but it was his imperfect judgment at the age of twenty which should be blamed. He had cast off his father's name, and with it his father's opinion of him. It was, he knew it was, his bid for liberty, Adler being in his mind the title of the species, Tommy the freedom of the person. But Wilky was his inescapable self.

In middle age you no longer thought such thoughts about free choice. Then it came over you that from one grandfather you had inherited such and such a head of hair . . . from another, broad thick shoulders. . . . Wandering races have such looks, the bone of one tribe, the skin of another. . . .

The changed name was a mistake [but] must his father continually remind him how he had sinned?

'Oh, God,'' Wilhelm prayed. . . . ''Have mercy.'' (25–6)

Moving back from a clearly insubstantial self (named Tommy), which is nothing more than fabrication and stage invention, to a more authentic self (named, by his father, Wilky), which carries forward the family genes (on all sides of the family, including the mother's), to an even more essential self (called in Yiddish Velvel), which is as much a pseudonym as Tommy but which places him within the tradition of peoplehood rather than just of family, Wilhelm does not arrive at a genuine "me." Rather he discovers himself (in Bellow's presentation of it) a part of a genealogy of shifting "monikers," none of which names him and all of which fix him in relation to someone else's idea of tradition: American, German, Jewish. The progression back from Tommy to Wilky to Velvel functions as an unraveling of Jewish history, from American assimilation to European assimilation to Yiddishkeit as its own form of assimilation: Does Wilhelm have a Hebrew name? And, if he did, what would be the status of such a name within Bellow's unwriting of Jewish genealogy, away from a moment of genuine creation or self-creation to what comes to be described by Wilhelm as a Babel-like "hell"?

Bellow plays at recovering essences, Jewish and otherwise, only to call into question the very idea of essential identity or "soul" – no less so in Jewish thought than in Emersonian individualism. Thus, to continue the line of Tamkin's Emersonian thought: As painful and dishonest as all the "pretender souls" that Wilhelm (like each of us, in one name or another) embodies, so is the "real soul" whom these pretenders seem to displace. "The true soul loves the truth," Tamkin explains. And therefore, "it wants to kill the pretender." And Tamkin continues, in a series of pronouncements that damn rather than celebrate the presumed "real" soul:

"The love has turned to hate. Then you become dangerous. A killer. You have to kill the deceiver. . . . Whenever the slayer slays, he wants to slay the soul in him which was gypped and deceived him. Who is his enemy? Him. And his lover? Also. Therefore, all suicide is murder, and all murder is suicide. It's the one and identical phenomenon."

As Wilhelm rightly concludes: "But this means that the world is full of murderers. So it's not the world. It's a kind of hell" (71).

What characterizes this hell of wholesale slaughter is, among other things, the sheer impossibility of separating out phenomena, of knowing who is killing whom, and why. Which is the soul that is gypped? Which the one who deceives? Who is the "he" who is "his" (whose?) enemy? What is pretend? And what is real? Given the context of the Holocaust in which this drama takes place, the book's European flavor, and its Jewish cast of characters, we cannot escape recognizing Tamkin's world full of murderers, his hell, as the modern post-Holocaust world. But if this is so, then Tamkin's confusion between real and pretender souls and his inability to distinguish murder from suicide has direct, and extremely repugnant, historical implications. For in the book's implicit retelling of Jewish history (its inversion of scripture or its new version thereof), it does not matter whether the real soul is Jewish (either biblically speaking or Yiddishly speaking or in some assimilated form) or whether it is Emersonian: In our deepest selves we are murderers all, whether we are murdering ourselves or others – which may not be a tenable distinction in any event. In Bellow's account, at least as we may extrapolate it from Tamkin's philosophy, we cannot tell the victimizers from the victims, the Nazis from the Jews. Whether this confusion is the consequence of the text's pervasive nihilism or the actual intention of its author is difficult to determine. But

101

Bellow would be neither the first nor the last to raise this specter of Jewish complicity in the Holocaust.

Bellow had earlier, in *The Victim*, provided a more sociological variety of this same argument. In this novel, the Jewish Asa Leventhal is falsely accused by a chronic antisemite of having willfully and maliciously caused the latter to lose his job in revenge for his antisemitism (as a descendant of New England wealth and position, Kirby Allbee, the antisemite, serves to implicate America itself in a kind of pervasive antisemitism). At first Leventhal resists this accusation. Gradually, however, he comes to accept it, making himself, in his own mind, less the victim of antisemitism than the victimizer of the antisemite – up until the moment Allbee tries to gas Leventhal (and perhaps himself – it's not clear) to death. Not only is the Jew, in the perverted logic of victim-victimizer that this story exposes, responsible for the ills (especially financial and spiritual) of the non-Jewish world, as the antisemite claims he is, but he wreaks his vengeance as a response to the world's antisemitism, which wholly galvanizes the Jew's sensibility, though he clearly ought not to have any response whatsoever to such Jew-baiting. Against the backdrop of the Holocaust, which the book clearly invokes through its references to the millions of Jews just killed, this not only verifies the Nazis' claims against the Jews, but makes the Jews after the war, with their heightened sensitivities to antisemitism, more dangerous still. Antisemitism, as the cause of Jewish misbehavior, is thus transformed, in the perverted logic of both Leventhal and Allbee, into an appropriate gauge of and response to Jewish villainy.

In *Seize the Day*, Bellow takes this argument concerning Jewish complicity in their own victimization one step further. Bellow's defense of "humanism" in *Seize the Day* (such as it is) is not, as some critics have claimed, in any way a defense of Judaism. Indeed, it is a powerful condemnation, not only of assimilated Jews, but of Judaism itself. For the object of Bellow's critique is the religious impulse (whether in the guise of Judaism or Christianity or Emersonianism), which imagines souls in the first place. As Tamkin explains, it is "for simplification purposes" that he has "spoken of the soul; it isn't a scientific term, but it helps you to understand it" (71). What it helps us to understand is that the object of Bellow's attack is the very concept of a *soul*, which is what binds all the Western theologies (Judaism and Christianity, and Emersonianism as well) together and makes them dangerous to modern humanity. Thus Bellow specifically includes Roman Catholicism in his panoply of failed and failing faiths. "Up in Roxbury," we are told, Tommy "had to go and explain to the priest, who was not sympathetic," and even though "Olive said she would marry him outside the Church when he was divorced," "she was beginning to dread his days in Roxbury." Even Olive's father, who "was a pretty decent old guy" and "said he understood what it is all about," feels compelled to "advise" Olive to give him up (94). "I'll try to start again with Olive," Tommy declares defiantly toward the end of the book, only to have his resolution dissolve, once again, into uncertainty: "In fact, I must. Olive loves me. Olive – " (115). Tommy Wilhelm can expect salvation from no one and no faith, not from his father or his lover or his ex-wife or his children or even from the philosopher-poet of the modern world, the psychologist Tamkin, who also cannot rid his vocabulary of the idea of a soul.

The alternative to the religious language of the modern world would seem to be the ancient and classical (Greek, Roman, Egyptian) counter-wisdom of pagan philosophy from which the novella takes its title: "The past is no good to us," explains Tamkin. "The future is full of anxiety. Only the present is real – the here-and-now. Seize the day" (66); and later: "You have to pick out something that's in the actual, immediate present moment . . . And say to yourself here-and-now, here-and-now, here-and-now. . . . Grasp the hour, the moment, the instant" (89–90). But this wisdom, which is said "as if in prayer" (90) and is expressed by that "confuser of the imagination," Tamkin (93), may no more be the truth of this book than the other systems of thought it replaces. For what characterizes "the great, great crowd, the inexhaustible current of millions of every race and kind, pouring out, pressing round, of every age, of every genius" if not just this futile and mindless conviction to seize the day, which is another, only another, variety of Emersonianism gone wild: *"I labor, I spend, I strive, I design, I love, I cling, I uphold, I give way, I envy, I long, I scorn, I die, I hide, I want"* (115)?

The funeral scene which concludes the novella, toward which Tommy is hurrying in the above passage, buries the wisdom of the philosophy that becomes the title of the book with as much finality as it buries all the other systems of belief it has raised. With the rifts between himself and his father and himself and his wife almost beyond repair and with Tamkin (his other father) gone, Wilhelm joins the funeral procession that provides him with his only moment of genuine release. Being buried in this scene and thus providing Tommy with his one moment of peace are both of Wilhelm's fathers and the paternal heritage they represent, including Judaism, Christianity, Emersonianism, Freudianism, and even the paganism of the book's title.

Seize the Day is a nihilistic book for which the central activity is neither worship nor daily practice but *mourning*. What occasions the need for mourning is, in this novel, the six million: the six million who are the victims, in Bellow's account, not simply of a Nazi aberration of western culture, or a Romantic twist of the moral sensibilities, or of the Christian heritage of antisemitism, or even of their own Jewishness (either in its willingness to assimilate to Romanticism and Christianity or in its refutation of them). Rather they are the victims of a two-millennium-long, worldwide history of the failure of theology and philosophy both, from classical times to our own.

What the modern world requires, from Bellow's point of view, is (as it were) the eradication of the world as we know it. In practical terms this means the unwriting of all the scriptures of the western theological and philosophical tradition and the self-restraint not to indulge in their rewriting. Hence, the passage I quoted at the beginning of this essay, Bellow's Genesis as Apocalypse, with its at first unfathomable emphasis on language, expressed, among other things, in its vision of the hell of the modern world as a kind of Tower of Babel. For Bellow the question is how human beings are to speak to one another and to make themselves understood, how fathers are to be fathers and sons, sons, without the infinitely laborious processes of translation and explanation getting in the way of even the simplest of human requests. For Bellow the project is to discover the path by which human beings move language, not beyond its limitations, but to a moment prior to its limitations, to a moment where what language speaks is human emotion rather than human thought.

The funeral for the unknown Jew, with which the novel concludes, provides the scene for Bellow's de-creation of the world as we know it, in which what is sacrificed, in order for a new world to be born, are self, language, and the world itself. "Moved forward by the pressure of the crowd . . . carried from the street into the chapel" and finally "past words, past reason, coherence," Tommy Wilhelm exactly *does not* consciously choose his final epiphanic experience but is ineluctably led toward it by the events of what the text calls "a day of reckoning" (123–5, 103). And as Tommy relinquishes the will either to direct his own actions or to save himself, he moves beyond self and language and into the realm of pure feeling:

His face swelled, his eyes shone hugely with instant tears. . . . The source of all tears had suddenly sprung open within him, black, deep, and hot, and they were pouring out and convulsed his body. . . . His efforts to collect himself were useless. The great knot of ill and grief in his throat swelled upward and he gave in utterly and held his face and wept. He cried with all his heart. . . . The flowers and lights fused ecstatically in Wilhelm's blind, wet eyes; the heavy sea-like music came up to his ears. It poured into him where he had hidden himself in the center of a crowd by the great and happy oblivion of tears. He heard it and sank deeper than sorrow, through torn sobs and cries toward the consummation of his heart's ultimate need. (117–18)

Numerous critics have suggested that Bellow transforms Judaism into a universalist, humanistic religion, thus preserving Jewish values even as he abandons recognizably Jewish beliefs and culture.[9] This idea ignores certain fundamental features of Bellow's art, which are nowhere more in evidence than in this funeral scene. In the first place, Tommy's experience at the funeral is far less Jewish than Christian. It is even Christ-like. His revelation and his salvation come together in his willingness to yield himself to an ecstatic fusion which results in the consummation of his heart's need. These are not Jewish but Christian images and terms, as are the references to the flowers, the open coffin, the pews, and the attire of the funeral goers, all of which suggest a more Christian than Jewish affair.[10] This is, perhaps, another reason that Bellow decided to blur the identity of the Jewish star in the funeral parlor. He wished to acknowledge the degree to which this is *not* a Jewish event, or, more precisely perhaps, not primarily or exclusively a Jewish event. But this is to say, as well, that Bellow's unknown Jew is now an unknown everyman, the victim of the world's recent barbarism being not only the Jews but all of us. An additional factor to be taken into account here is that Bellow textually revises the star in the years following the publication of *Mr. Sammler's Planet*. In this more deliberately Holocaust novel, Bellow mounts an attack against the survivors of both the Holocaust and slavery. The Jew (as Israeli) and the black, in Bellow's view, have both transformed victimhood into special pleading and power and have now made themselves into the victimizers of others. In the barbarism of contemporary New York City and the State of Israel, repetitions of past atrocities make history to bear, with excruciating painfulness, on the present moment.[11]

For this reason, as the abundant water imagery surrounding the funeral in *Seize the Day* suggests, the funeral is a scene of dissolution, the flood, preparatory to the reconstitution of the world on some other terms, though what those terms are, Bellow's new scripture does not specify. If it is humanism, then one must at least say that, preceding humanism, in Bellow's view, is nihilism, that before one can construct a truly human world one must completely discard the world that has come before: One must mourn it, bury it, and perhaps even say a *yizkor* prayer for it, but one cannot resurrect it or reconstruct it or in any way utilize the materials or the languages of its self-conception.

For this reason, it seems to me important that the story take place neither on the day of Atonement nor on the eve of the day of Atonement. Atonement, in this story, is still at some undefined moment in the future. It will come after mourning, and although atonement will be a self-conscious activity, it will not be a particularly Jewish one. Such days of reckoning as exist will no longer be bound by tradition. They will be private and personal and will no longer participate in the systems of thought that have heretofore defined the civilized world as we know it.

NOTES

1   The major psychoanalytic study of the book is Daniel Weiss, "Caliban on Prospero: A Psychoanalytic Study on the Novel *Seize the Day*, by Saul Bellow," in *Saul Bellow and the Critics*, ed. Irving Malin (New York: New York University Press, 1967), pp. 114–41; see also John J. Clayton, "Saul Bellow's *Seize the Day*: A Study in Mid-Life Transition," *Saul Bellow Journal* 5 (1986): 34–47; J. Brooks Bouson, "The Narcissistic Self-Drama of Wilhelm Adler: A Kohutian Reading of Bellow's *Seize the Day*, " *Saul Bellow Journal* 5 (1986): 3–14; Daniel Fuchs, *Saul Bellow: Vision and Revision* (Durham, NC: Duke University Press, 1984), pp. 79–82; and Harold Fisch, "Bellow and Kafka," in *Saul Bellow: A Mosaic*, ed. L. H. Goldman, Gloria L. Cronin, and Ada Aharoni (New York: Peter Lang, 1992), who gives the Oedipal reading a more literary ambience by reading the father-son conflict as not only recalling Kafka's same use of this theme but as also evidencing Bellow's relationship to his literary forefather; see also Weiss, "Caliban on Prospero," in this regard.

2   The passage that is being misread, both by Gaye McCollum Simmons in "Atonement in Bellow's *Seize the Day*," *Saul Bellow Journal* 11/12 (1993/4): 30–53 and by Daniel Weiss in "Caliban on Prospero," is:
Rappaport [addressed] a few remarks to Wilhelm. He asked him whether he had reserved his seat in the synagogue for Yom Kippur.
"No," said Wilhelm.
"Well, you better hurry up if you expect to say *Yiskor* for your parents. I never miss." (86)

3   Saul Bellow, *It All Adds Up: From the Dim Past to the Uncertain Future* (London: Sacker and Warburg, 1994), p. 312.

4   On this point, see, for example, L. H. Goldman, "The Jewish Perspective of Saul Bellow," *Saul Bellow: A Mosaic*, ed. L. H. Goldman, Gloria L. Cronin, and Ada Aharoni (New York: Peter Lang, 1992), 3–19 and S. Lillian Kremer's discussion of Bellow's Holocaust fiction in *Witness Through the Imagination: Jewish American Holocaust Literature* (Detroit: Wayne State University Press, 1989), pp. 36–62.

5   For an informed set of recent essays on this subject see *Probing the*

Limits of Representation: Nazism and the "Final Solution," ed. Saul Friedländer (Cambridge: Harvard University Press, 1992). The question of representability is a pervasive one in Holocaust studies.

6 I have discussed these issues at greater length in: "Lionel Trilling and the 'Being' of Culture," *The Massachusetts Review*, 35 (1994): 63–82; "The Holocaust and the Construction of Modern American Literary Criticism: The Case of Lionel Trilling," *The Translatability of Cultures: Figurations of the Space Between*, ed. Sanford Budick and Wolfgang Iser (Stanford: Stanford University Press, 1995), pp. 127–46; "The Haunted House of Fiction: Ghostwriting the Holocaust," *Common Knowledge* 5 (1996): 120–35; "Acknowledging the Holocaust in Contemporary American Fiction and Criticism," forthcoming, *Breaking Crystal: Memory and Writing after Auschwitz*, ed. Efraim Sicher (Illinois University Press, 1997); and "Silent Inscriptions of the Holocaust in American Literary Culture," *Living with America, 1946–1996*, ed. Christina Giorcelli and Rob Kroes (Amsterdam: VU University Press, 1997), 191–210.

7 Compare L. H. Goldman, "The Jewish Perspective of Saul Bellow," particularly the discussion of Bellow, Judaism, humanism, Romanticism, and Nazism, pp. 8–19.

8 Compare such statements as, in Emerson's "Self-Reliance": "Trust thyself" (148); "Society everywhere is in conspiracy against the manhood of every one of its members" (149); or the section on charity (150), in *Selections from Ralph Waldo Emerson*, ed. Stephen E. Whicher (Boston: Houghton Mifflin), 1960. In Thoreau's *Walden*: "It is hard to have a Southern overseer; it is worse to have a Northern one; but worst of all when you are the slave-driver of yourself. . . . The mass of men live lives of quiet desperation" (4–5). *Walden*, introduction, Norman Holmes Person (New York: Holt, Rinehart and Winston).

9 See, for example, Simmons, "Atonement," p. 30, and L. H. Goldman, "The Jewish Perspective of Saul Bellow: "The 'quality' of Bellow's Jewishness is incontrovertible. Saul Bellow's perspective is unmistakably Jewish. Throughout his *oeuvre*, which comprises his 'song of songs,' his humanistic voice intones the anthropocentric concerns of his heritage" (19). A more realistic projection of Bellow's Jewishness is Sarah Blacher Cohen's in *Saul Bellow's Enigmatic Laughter* (Urbana: University of Illinois Press, 1974), pp. 90–114, in which Cohen discusses *Seize the Day* in terms of the Jewish archetypes and figures it evokes.

10 Concerning the influence of American Christian practice on Jewish

funerals, see Janna Weissman Joselit, *The Wonders of America: Reinventing Jewish Culture 1880–1950* (New York: Hill and Wang, 1996), pp. 265–95 and Samuel H. Dresner, *The Jew in American Life* (New York: Crown Publishers, Inc., 1963), pp. 20–49.

11 I develop this argument in my chapter on *Mr. Sammler's Planet* in *Blacks and Jews in Literary Conversation*, forthcoming. For a more sustained discussion of his views on Israel, see Bellow's *To Jerusalem and Back*, and my own commentary on this work in: "*To Jerusalem and Back*: Reflections on the Place of Israel in American Writing from Melville and Mark Twain to Saul Bellow," *South Central Review* 8 (1991): 59–70.

6

Death and the Post-Modern Hero/Schlemiel:
An Essay on *Seize the Day*

JULES CHAMETZKY

W HO CAN TAKE Tommy Wilhelm seriously? "Ass! Idiot! Wild boar, dumb mule! Slave! Lousy, wallowing hippopotamus!" (55) he says of himself, and who can disagree? The occasion was the first time his dad, that "healthy and fine small old man," refuses to give him the money he desperately needs. Dr. Adler is something of a case, a vain old eagle ashamed of his son, thinking "what a Wilky he has given the world" – but more on him later. Enough to know that he sees that Tommy (the new)/Wilky (the old, or "traditional") is a slob – which he is, despite the Jack Fagman shirt. Note the cigarette butts and debris in his pockets, the grime left on the egg white when he peels his morning egg. His father knows he's a lousy driver, evasive and rationalizing about losing his job, a fool to trust Dr. Tamkin, a loser. Tamkin knows a fish, too, and plays him expertly. In Tommy's eyes his estranged wife Margaret is choking him to death with her implacability, but she has reason and motherhood (1950s style) on her side, and she was no ogre when she nursed him with poetry through his Hollywood flu. Even the minor players take his measure – Rubin the newsdealer knows and knows and knows, as does the clerk in the brokerage house. To the ox-like pimp Maurice Venice and the wealthy chicken killer Mr. Rappaport he's a nobody, really, a possible means to small ends. So what is he if he is not just a *yold* – a fool?

A case can be made for that, and some have suggested it – one more in the line of holy fools, *schlemiels* serving god and man as the world, which is after all *tref*, regards them as foolish.[1] They suffer, but display humility in the face of the great, sad human spectacle generally touching (and flattering) our own humanity.

111

Tommy has an epiphany in the subway, feeling his oneness with all the "imperfect and disfigured . . . lurid-looking" people, and at the end, his tears for a dead stranger can be seen simultaneously for himself and every man. And so it goes. Tommy Wilhelm/Wilky Adler may ultimately be a *Velvel*, but he is no *Gimpel Tam* – as in the I. B. Singer story Bellow so brilliantly translated shortly before *Seize the Day* (see Wirth-Nesher's chapter in this volume) and if anyone knows a hawk from a handsaw it is Saul Bellow. Wilky does have redeeming features, but he's too responsible for his own miseries and mistakes, and although the final flood of tears ends the story well – may even provide a kind of catharsis – it does not (as Budick suggests) necessarily constitute a broader redemptive move.

Let's talk first about what a terrific writer Bellow is, then about less and more important matters: money and speculation (all that is solid melts in the air), memory and desire, fathers and sons, death (singular and massive) and the self.

1

The detail. The first time we see Dr. Adler, he's sprinkling sugar on his strawberries – while Wilky pops cokes and pills. Later, Tamkin's Yankee pot roast and cabbage, and two cups of coffee, in the cafeteria with the gilded front are memorably lurid. In contrast to the self-satisfied carnivore, Tommy has a yogurt and crackers with tea, an echo of the *Ur*-anti-hero of modernism Leopold Bloom, who eats cheese and no meat for lunch after seeing cattle led through the Dublin streets toward the shambles. Tommy has just reflected in the brokerage house on the source of old Rappaport's presumed wealth – "the sinister business" of chickens being slaughtered, "animals in their millions . . . the blood filling the Gulf of Mexico. The chicken shit, acid, burning the earth" (85).

That knowledge is etched in us all, but we move on, in our urbs covering over the old killing sites with parks and grass, pushing them to the margins of our cities and consciousness. The story of civilization in a sentence. Bellow reserves his best arias (a term he used for wonderfully written sections of his five-issues late-sixties journal *The Noble Savage*) for descriptions of New York. We remember the opening of *The Victim* where the city in summer takes on the exotic quality of Bangkok. Here it is the upper West Side, where the old used to live, that is given its definitive stamp. From the open window of the Hotel Gloriana (what literary echoes the name evokes![2]) Tommy sees a pigeon alight on the chain holding up the movie marquee below and "for one moment he heard the wings beat strongly" (4). The *malech ha movis* (the angel of death) passing over (or landing at?) the house of the Israelites while the first-born son looks on anxiously? Meanwhile, the newsdealer in his "rich brown suit" and Countess Mara necktie is looking "dreamily" down the street toward the Hotel Ansonia, built by Stanford White "like a baroque palace from Prague or Munich enlarged a hundred times . . . [but with] black television antennae . . . densely planted on its round summits" (5). In a few sentences rich with observed detail of a specific time, place, class, ethnicity (as we would say now – note the shirt that needed dry cleaning and cost Wilhelm "sixteen, eighteen bucks," top of the line then) Bellow lifts us with easy allusiveness and intertextuality into the larger world of western culture, history, myth.

His famous combination of vernacular and high-style, street smarts and the Harvard five-foot shelf, was the breakthrough achievement of *The Adventures of Augie March* three years earlier. But toward the end of that long book the manner could seem to be forced, the energy of the crackling sentences imposed, a *shtick* whose technique became too discernible. Perhaps Bellow's voice is best in the shorter and more meditative pieces. Certainly in *Seize the Day* his central character's consciousness (compare Henry James's prefaces[3]) – and all those who pass into and through it – are brought to life with short, vivid descriptions and snatches of perfect dialogue: perfect although always a little off-center, unusual in their vocabularies, frequently intellectually and rhetorically pretentious, reflective, all clearly Bellow's people. Undoubtedly, like Wilhelm, a part of Bellow was a sucker for madmen like Tamkin, who populate his stories, with grandiose schemes about humankind (or the market). Even Wilhelm recognizes him as a fraud, what "a real jerk" he must be to listen to Tamkin's preposterous stories and notions, but he confesses to being "a real sucker for people who talk about the deeper things of life, even the way he does." The difference is that Tommy places his fate in Tamkin's hands, *against* the keener sense of reality that is also always present to him as he reflects on his life. That is his pattern – knowing all the reasons he *shouldn't* take a certain course of action but then doing it. A mess of contradictions, "all balled up" he says of himself at the end of the first section, asking for mercy as he is going in to breakfast with his father – who will reject his pleas.

Bellow himself was physically more like Dr. Adler than like Wilky, slight, fine-boned, elegant rather than a large, shambling, awkward type like Asa Leventhal in *The Victim* or Tommy Wilhelm. Psychically? He contains them all. If Flaubert could say of Emma Bovary, *c'est moi*, let's allow Bellow the same authority. He knows how messed up people and the world are – the act of writing is an effort at equilibrium, a balancing act carried on in the midst of contending forces that offer no easy way to live one's life. Wilhelm the character contains multiple (at least three) selves, others from without clamoring for attention, or threatening his precarious grip on any kind of self at all – the drama of a drowning man (the imagery of sinking beneath watery surfaces is pervasive) grasping for an ever elusive, steady lifeline.

The seven sections of the novella are marvelously organized, no big or necessary scene avoided, all flowing inevitably in their "day of reckoning" (note the classical unities) in which Wilhelm expects to confront a real truth about himself and his life. In the second section, we see the old animosities, the Oedipal struggle with the father reemerging, the father's aversion for the son made manifest (what a Wilky he had given the world – "Wilhelm lived in worse filth than a savage," see Weber and Girgus in this volume) although in the temporary presence of a third party, the former refugee Mr. Perls, this doesn't flair up totally, as it does in the next section when they are alone together. At first, the date of the mother's death, "the beginning of the end," which only Wilky gets right is established ("toward 1934"). Thereafter, the father who doesn't "like the mention of death" flatly rejects Wilhelm's appeal for money and the painful scene ends with Tommy crying out miserably. "Just keep your money."

The fourth section belongs to Wilhelm and the other Doctor/ Father in his life, Tamkin, who does not eschew emotion. It's long, complex, funny and sad, brilliant. Tamkin immediately puts him off balance with his first line, "You have a very obsessional look on your face." This refutes, yet once more, Wilhelm's conception of himself. In the first line of the story describing him it is said "when it came to concealing his troubles, Tommy Wilhelm was not less capable than the next fellow." He believes he can hide behind his hat and cigar and an impassive demeanor, but he is actually volatile, transparent; everyone sees through him. To Tamkin, in any case, *nothing* is as it appears to be. Everyone has a secret, carries a concealed desire or mental disorder (63). He, of course, claims to have the key to the secrets, even of the future (at least in the commodities market). The past is no good for us, he says as he rolls out his incredible stories, the future full of anxiety: He preaches "the real universe," the here and now. "Seize the day!" (66) Coming from such a source the sermon is immediately suspect.

Tommy sees much of this as Tamkin's bull-throwing, the contradictions glaringly apparent. He notes astutely that those people climbing Mt. Everest were also seizing the day on the slopes and surely at the top, not content to remain passive at the base of Tamkin's poetic Mt. Serenity/Everest. He sees that the poem is claptrap and illiterate (why forth? "why-forth is wrong") and by the end of the section wonders what he has let himself in for. Yet he follows him.

Tamkin displays energy and certainty – and he makes Tommy *laugh*, as in his story about the nudist-dentist in riding pants and boots and green eyeshade. Significantly Tamkin touches Wilhelm's sense of his own duality – "the description of the two souls . . . awed him. In Tommy he saw the pretender, and even Wilky might not be himself. Might the true name of his true soul be the one by which his grandfather had called him – Velvel?" (72). A powerful passage. To any student of ethnicity in America an "aha!" experience: The third generation returning to the first to find and restore an important part of the self that the second generation rejected ("we were *nothing*," back there in Willamsburg as poor immigrants says the second generation Dr. Adler).[4] In the context of the 1950s Jewish American writers' "breakthrough" into the mainstream even as they discovered and celebrated their Jewishness, this is valid enough, though treated lightly and tempered by the uncertainty of Wilhelm's character and milieu. More to the point is Wilhelm's character as another of Bellow's dangling men, between realities, an armored personality, really, as revealed in the tightening of his shoulders and the constriction in his chest, a candidate as much for Wilhelm Reich (another of Bellow's enthusiasms at one time) as for ethnic rooting. Nor will "water and exercise," his ethnically cleansed father's prescription for what ails him, release the flow of energy and hope that Tamkin temporarily does. It's all funny and not funny, true but false, here today/gone tomorrow.

And so to the market, where the lamb is led to his slaughter. Like all those chickens. But first he reflects that in New York there is only one's self to talk to (and we have seen what an uncertain entity that is), "that everybody is an outcast." There is, however, "a larger body" beneath "the details" (84). Details of what, one asks, remembering Herzog's great query in response to Heidegger's fear of "falling into the quotidian" – "where, Dr. Heidegger, did you fall from?"[5] Tommy yearns for, perhaps discerns briefly, a place "the true soul" can talk to, where "sons and fathers are themselves" – a wonderful, plaintive line. But Bellow distrusts the mad search for transcendence, up or down, a distrust he shared with early critics of Heidegger like Theodor Adorno (whose views hover over this text, for me, in a suggestive fashion), like Tamkin in his rhetoric a champion of the here and now, "the real universe." There is, once again, ambiguity here.

But the market – unpredictable, driven by hope and fear – and failure do deliver clear verdicts. Tommy Wilhelm's lard futures are liquidated, he's wiped out (as they say). All that is solid, and so forth – impermanence, flux, insubstantiality rule the day. He wants to cry but cannot here, in "the crowded theater of the brokerage house" (that simulacrum of "real life"). He will achieve his tears and catharsis, if that is what it is, only in the theater of the funeral parlor – face to face with real death, the only truly inimitable thing.

Before that climactic moment he searches unsuccessfully for the missing Tamkin, confronts his father again, this time in the steam room beneath the Gloriana – a scene out of Fellini – some kind of hell, though for Dr. Adler the scene of life-giving water and touch (the rubdown). Tommy had said to Tamkin that the world is full of murder, "a kind of hell," to which Tamkin replied, "At least a kind of purgatory. You can walk on the bodies" (71). Here Dr. Adler rejects/kills him again, then he has a fateful call from Margaret who rejects unequivocally his plea for time/ relenting/mercy. At the end of his rope, Wilhelm stumbles on a funeral a few blocks away, mistakenly thinks he sees the elusive Tamkin, stands by the open casket of a complete stranger, and weeps deeply. Was he the dead man's brother (remember the subway epiphany), the onlookers ask, his grief is so great! No, they don't look alike. Of course he's crying for himself – and more. As the heavy, sea-like music (the sinking to a watery death motif throughout) comes up to his ears. "He heard it and sank deeper than sorrow, through torn sobs and cries toward the consummation of his heart's ultimate need."

Thus the story ends, on that great line – beautifully led up to, as I hope I have indicated, unfolding feelingly, ideas and all. But what, precisely, does it mean? What is "deeper than sorrow?" What is "the consummation of his heart's ultimate need?"

2

One can say at once, off the top of one's head, as it were, that he is expressing his delayed mourning – his *yizkor* – for the absent mother and his own status as an outcast and orphan in the universe. On another level, one must agree with Mark Shechner and Emily Budick who find it is "the sorrow that dare not speak its name" – the Holocaust that illuminates the grief and the emotional landscape of the story. Shechner most insightfully finds in *Dangling Man* and later books that take up its mood "a literature of mourning." Joseph K. feels "a sorrow for deaths he cannot name or number and therefore openly mourn,'' a sorrow which Shechner suggests Bellow finally ''works through'' in Tommy Wilhelm's tears in *Seize the Day*.[6] The work is no doubt ''Holocaust-inflected'' as Budick has said of postwar American Jewish writing, from Bellow's fiction to Lionel Trilling's criticism, though obliquely and not directly confronted – for reasons Budick demonstrates persuasively.[7] I would argue, however, that as the horrible and final catastrophe of an ''age of enormity'' (in Isaac Rosenfeld's phrase),[8] the Holocaust reduced to rubble most ideological, teleological, transcendent notions of the human condition (once a fighting word) and its destiny. In the same year as *Dangling Man*, Theodor Adorno wrote in an addendum to his *Minima Moralis* (subtitled ''Reflections on a Damaged Life''):

To think that after this war life can return to ''normal,'' or that culture can be ''built up again'' . . . is idiotic. Millions of Jews have been murdered – as if that were an ''entr' acte'' and not the catastrophe itself. . . . Death is normal.[9]

The Holocaust (not so called until the Eichmann trial in 1963) cast its shadow broadly. The whole question of an ineluctable reality separate from horror and of an impermeable self is thrown into permanent crisis, along with western culture and its pretensions. ''The new philosophy casts all in doubt/all coherence gone,'' wrote John Donne of the split between the medieval and the modern world. The explosion of violence, slaughter, and death of the Second World War must be considered the end of modernity, the beginning (forget 1968) of post-modernity. All is in doubt, flux, contingent, cultural efforts mere *briccolage*, language a solace but no sure correction to ''our heart's ultimate need.'' The only fixed reality is death itself. *Seize the Day* is death-haunted, Holocaust-inflected, certainly insofar as it gave us a world in which *Normal ist der Tod*.

The culture exhausted, discredited, the abyss clearly discernible to all thinking people, the popularity of Existentialism in those years can be understood. But Bellow was/is no Existentialist. He decries more than once in his critical writings intellectual handwringing and fashionable *angst*. The 1952 *Partisan Review* symposium on ''Our Country and Our Culture'' and Bellow's

Augie March the next year marked an end to "alienation" in those quarters and a "return to America" in an optative mood. But "the great weight of the unspoken" is still there and in Bellow that mood did not seem to last long.

Bellow, like some of his most memorable characters in the early work – Joseph K., Asa Leventhal, Tommy Wilhelm – seems to exist between options and realities making insistent demands on him, more or less in a liminal state. Such an indeterminate position allows reflections on questions of identity and self, issues avoided in "ordinary" life. Thus the richness of the texts, but also a precarious state as well as a privileged one in which no action or commitment is to be made. Leventhal in *The Victim* is rescued from the madness of his liminal condition when his wife returns, summer is over, the cloths removed from the furniture, and ordinary life resumed. In his liminal effort to come to terms with his past, who he is, and what he now desires, Wilhelm is from a very important view admirable – his self-reflection a redeeming feature as compared with the false fathers – but the only way he can leave his liminality is by facing death.

"A man is only as good as what he loves," Wilhelm once heard a "guy" say, and thinks it a profound statement. What does Dr. Adler love? *Peace*, he says, which seems to mean not giving money to his needy children, being left alone to enjoy the hedonistic comforts of his fastidious life. Tamkin says he loves *everybody* – which is the same as saying nobody. Two great egoists. And Tommy Wilhelm? The absent mother looms large – whose grave he visits, decrying the vandals' desecration of this holy place, whose death was the beginning of the end. If that was the alpha, the omega was the death of patriarchy – Tamkin (Tamkin!) calling Dr. Adler "a fine old patriarch" (62) and sinister Rappaport "a regular patriarch" (97) writes *finis* to the whole concept.

Wilhelm reflects on his own sons and his relation to them, realizing that with them "he was not himself . . . [and] a weary heaviness came over him" (93–4). The story can be read as about the end of patriarchy (along with other "fixed" belief systems) and perhaps a kind of mourning for that. We now inhabit a world in which "the fathers were no fathers and the sons no sons," and only in some ideal realm of "the real soul" are "sons and fathers . . . themselves." Bellow writes movingly and often on this theme, so one cannot lightly dismiss the wistful yearning/mourning in it.

And what does a man fear? Dr. Adler fears death. He does not want to hear about it, although in denying Tommy aid he says he'll be dead soon enough and he doesn't want to be taken "for every buck," so get off my back! No Lear he. Surely we're in the realm of tragicomedy, not tragedy. Tamkin fears exposure of his fraudulence. Like one of Dante's most damned, he is a counterfeiter (of *personae*), a fraud, a deceiver and seducer – already in hell, dead. If Tommy wants or loves anything substantial it appears to be to nestle himself like a child in Olive's maternal, Catholic embrace – a hopeless pietà of an image which, though sensuous, is already half in love with easeful death.

Tommy remembers a snatch of poetry – "Love that well which thou must leave ere long" – and thinks at first that it refers to his father, "but then he understood that it was for himself, rather" (12). That seems to argue for life, since "everyone this side of the grave is the same distance from death" (45). He argues with his father that the threat of death does not release us from obligations in life; it primarily means we're all close to death, every minute. Tommy will not be spared, does not spare himself – "the peculiar burden of his existence lay upon him like an accretion, a load, a hump" (39). That burden is his sense of orphanhood in the world, an outcast such as he dreams everyone is. And all those dead Jews? Certainly. And millions of others.

Although everyone (except Olive and her priest) are Jews in the story, the Jewishness is rather attenuated, the word "Jews" appearing only once or twice, as when Tamkin says "they" don't like Jews out there on the road (no response from Tommy [81]). A stab is made at distinguishing Jews based on religion: His mother was Reform, his father had no religion. Rappaport asks him if he's reserved a seat for Yom Kippur (Conservative? Orthodox?). There is no mention of Israel, no Zionism. (See Kramer and Budick in this volume.) Is this more evasion, the burden of things that can't be talked about? Perhaps – but then there is no politics or history, either, in any *direct* sense.

If there is only an oblique, at best, acknowledgment of the Holocaust, there is the broader historical context, well known to a generation of Jewish secular, humanist, anti-Stalinist leftist intellectuals to which Bellow (and Trilling and Rosenfeld, and all the others) belonged and by which he was shaped. These people lived through the dashed hopes of Socialism, betrayed by the brutalities of Stalin – the Ukraine massacres, the Purge Trials, Trotsky's assassination, the killing of Jewish writers and intellectuals – of the Depression, the Spanish Civil War, the rise and threat of fascism, the explosion of cataclysmic violence in the Second World War, *la bomba atomica*. A few years before *Seize the Day* there were the Rosenberg trial and execution, Stalin's death, and the spared Jewish doctors; in the year of its publication there were Suez, the Khrushchev revelations, and the Hungarian uprising. And there was no mention of *any* of these events, by a writer who was the first major American novelist who was a true intellectual, nurtured in his formative years in a milieu of the left and of intellectual journals, in full knowledge of the great issues and tragedies of his time.

Back to the ending. Bellow needed a strong one to a story that was wrapped in ambiguities, a release of sorts. The ambiguities result partly from his refusal to write a vulgarly socially "aware" or realist fiction (see the criticisms of his complicated view of antisemitism in *The Victim*) but rather one compact with ideas woven into a texture of sharply observed reality. Part of his idea structure was/is that the idea of "culture" itself, if not forever engulfed by the great wave of history recently negotiated, had to be reconstituted on a less grandiose basis – clear-eyed and honest, self-aware and sorrowful, but not self-pitying and self-glorifying. Mr. Sammler's planet had already gone under in 1944, and would seem to be doing so again in 1968. Maybe there are other planets somewhere, but as survivors all in 1956 (and now) we find there is still this planet to be lived on, however temporarily. There are no Fathers (no "World of . . ."[10]) to bail one out, redemption-wise, no consoling ideologies, history and culture in tatters (or at least under the shadow of TV *antennae*). The world may be *tref* – Wilhelm allows for the possibility – but there is no other sanctified reality. In the face of death, the only absolute, the end of Selfhood dialectically affirms that there is a Self, all erosions to the contrary notwithstanding. Death is normal.[11] Sad but true. Seize the day.

Balancing between memory and desire, between a fouled up, ungraspable past and futures that disappear in an eyeblink, stuck on earth with no transcendence up or down in sight, hoping for a healing touch that is more than a locker-room rubdown, the postmodern hero/anti-hero, *schlemiel* that he is has no choice but to weep and live on, one day after the other.

NOTES

1 See Ruth Wisse, *The Schlemiel as Modern Hero* (Chicago: University of Chicago Press, 1971) and Sanford Pinsker, *The Schlemiel as Metaphor* (Carbondale: University of Southern Illinois Press, 1971).

2 Edmund Spenser refers to Queen Elizabeth I as "Gloriana" in the *Faerie Queene*, and it is frequently used to refer to her in Elizabethan literature. For me, there is an echo in Henry James's *The Ambassadors*, in which the Italian artist Gloriani exerts an erotic and exotic power.

3 In his discussion of *Portrait of a Lady*. The prefaces are collected in Henry James, *The Art of the Novel* (New York: Scribners, 1962).

4 See Marcus Lee Hansen, "The Problem of the Third Generation," in Werner Sollors, ed., *Theories of Ethnicity: A Classical Reader* (New York: New York University Press, 1996), pp. 202–15.

5 Saul Bellow, *Herzog* (New York: Viking, 1964), p. 49.

6 Mark Shechner, "Jewish Writers," in Daniel Hoffman, ed., *Harvard Guide to Contemporary American Writing* (Cambridge: Harvard University Press, 1979), p. 201. See also p. 196, where Shechner cites Rosenfeld calling the period climaxing in world war and "the slaughter of the Jews," "an age of enormity."

7 See Budick's essay preceding in this volume and, for specific references, see her n. 5.

8 See Isaac Rosenfeld, *An Age of Enormity* (Cleveland: World Publishing, 1962). This volume was published posthumously, Rosenfeld

having died in 1956 at the age of 38. Bellow wrote an introduction for the volume.

9 Theodor W. Adorno, "Nachtrag zu den *Minima Moralis*," in *Vermischte Schriften* II (Suhrkamp Verlag: Frankfurt a/M, 1986), pp. 811–12. The German reads: "Der Gedanke, dass noch diesem krieg das leben "normal" weitergehen oder gar die kultur "wiederaufgebaut" werden Könnte – als wäre nicht der Wiederaufbau von kultur allein schon deren Negation – , ist idiotisch. Millionen Juden seid ermordet worden, und das soll ein Zwischenspeil sein und nicht die katastrophe selbst. . . . Normal is der Tod."

10 The reference is to Irving Howe, *World of Our Fathers: The Journey of East European Jews to America and the Life They Found and Made* (New York: Harcourt Brace Jovanovich, 1976).

11 Besides Adorno, T. S. Eliot's lines from "Chorus from 'The Rock' " may be relevant here, apropos of Wilhelm's confrontation with "the stranger": "When the stranger says, 'what is the meaning of this city?/ Do you huddle together because you love each other?' " [and ends] "Life you may evade, but Death you shall not./You shall not deny the Stranger" (*Collected Poems, 1919–1962* [London: Faber and Faber, 1963], p. 171). I am grateful to Werner Sollors for calling my attention to this reference. See also Julia Kristeva, *Strangers to Ourselves* (New York: Columbia University Press, 1991), chapter 3, "The Chosen People and the Choice of Forgiveness."

Notes on Contributors

Emily Miller Budick is Professor of American Studies at the Hebrew University of Jerusalem. Among her many publications are *Emily Dickinson and the Life of Language: A Study in Symbolic Poetics*; *Fiction and Historical Consciousness: The American Romance Tradition*; *Engendering Romance: Women Writers and the Hawthorne Tradition, 1850–1990*; *Nineteenth-Century American Romance: Genre and the Democratic Construction of Culture*; and the forthcoming *Blacks and Jews in Literary Conversation*. She is currently working on a book about Jewish-American and Israeli writers.

Jules Chametzky is editor of *The Massachusetts Review*. He has taught English and Humanities at the University of Minnesota, Boston University and, since 1958, at the University of Massachusetts in Amherst, where he is currently Professor Emeritus. He has also been a visiting professor and Fulbright Professor of American Literature at half a dozen European universities. He is author of *From the Ghetto: The Fiction of Abraham Cahan* and *Our Decentralized Literature: Cultural Mediations in Jewish and Southern Writers* and editor of Cahan's *The Rise of David Levinsky*.

Sam B. Girgus is Professor of English at Vanderbilt University. His most recent book is *Hollywood Renaissance: The Cinema of Democracy in the Era of Ford, Capra, and Kazan*. He is also the author of *The Films of Woody Allen*; *Desire and the Political Unconscious in American Literature*; *The New Covenant: Jewish Writers and the American Idea*; and *The Law of the Heart: Individualism and the Modern Self in American Literature*, as well as many articles and reviews on American culture, literature, and film. He also has edited several books, including *The American Self: Myth, Ideology, and Popular Culture*. He has held a Rockefeller Humanities Fellowship and a Senior Fulbright Fellowship, has lectured in many countries around the world, and has recently been awarded the Uppsala Fulbright Chair in American Studies at Uppsala University, Sweden.

Michael P. Kramer is Associate Professor of English at Bar-Ilan University. He has taught previously at the University of California, Davis and has been Senior Fulbright Lecturer and Visiting Professor at the Hebrew University of Jerusalem. He is the author of *Imagining Language in America, From the Revolution to the Civil War* and is currently at work on a book about theories of Jewishness in American thought and writing.

Donald Weber is Professor of English and American Literature at Mount Holyoke College. He has twice been a National Endowment for the Humanities Fellow, as well as a Woodrow Wilson Center for International Scholars Fellow. He is the author of *Rhetoric and History in Revolutionary New England*, along with numerous articles and reviews on American literature and culture, and is currently at work on a book about ethnic expression in American culture.

Hana Wirth-Nesher is Associate Professor of English at Tel Aviv University and Coordinator of the Samuel L. and Perry Haber Chair on the Study of the American Jewish Experience. She is the author of *City Codes: Reading the Modern Urban Novel* and of numerous essays on British, American, and Jewish literature. She is editor of *What is Jewish Literature?*, *The Sheila Carmel Lectures*, and, in *The American Novel* series, *New Essays on Call It Sleep*. She is currently at work on a book about multilingualism in Jewish-American literature.

Selected Bibliography

Editions

Seize the Day was originally published in *Partisan Review* 23 (Summer 1956). That same year it was published in book form by Viking Press as part of a collection called *Seize the Day and Other Stories*. Since then, the novel has appeared in several paperback editions and may be found as well in *The Portable Saul Bellow* and *The Norton Anthology of American Literature*. An edition "with author's corrections" was published by Penguin Books in 1975. This edition has been reprinted many times, most recently in 1996 with an introduction by Cynthia Ozick. Unless otherwise noted, this is the edition quoted by the authors in this collection.

Bibliographies

Cronin, Gloria L., and Blaine H. Hall. *Saul Bellow: An Annotated Bibliography*, second edition. New York: Garland Publishing, 1987.

Noreen, Robert G. *Saul Bellow: A Reference Guide*. Boston: G. K. Hall, 1978.

Sokoloff, B. A., and Mark E. Posner. *Saul Bellow: A Comprehensive Bibliography*, updated edition. Belfast, ME: Bern Porter, 1985.

Biography

Miller, Ruth. *Saul Bellow: A Biography of the Imagination*. New York: St. Martin's Press, 1991.

Criticism

For articles on *Seize the Day* published before 1987, the reader is referred to the bibliographies listed above. A good continuing source for articles

Selected Bibliography

on *Seize the Day* is the *Saul Bellow Journal,* which is published semi-annually. (Before 1982, the journal was known as the *Saul Bellow Newsletter.*) Included below are selected recent articles on *Seize the Day* published in other journals, along with book-length studies and collections of essays on Bellow and his work. Not included are critical works already referred to in the notes to the essays in this volume.

Bloom, Harold, ed. *Saul Bellow.* Modern Critical Views. New York: Chelsea House, 1986.

Bradbury, Malcolm. *Saul Bellow.* Contemporary Writers. London: Methuen, 1982.

Braham, Jeanne. *A Sort of Columbus: The American Voyages of Saul Bellow's Fiction.* Athens: University of Georgia Press, 1984.

Clayton, John Jacob. *Saul Bellow: In Defense of Man.* Bloomington: Indiana University Press, 2nd ed., 1979.

Costello, Patrick. "Tradition in *Seize the Day,*" *Essays in Literature* 14 (1987), 117–31.

Cronin, Gloria L., and L. H. Goldman, eds. *Saul Bellow in the 1980s: A Collection of Critical Essays.* East Lansing: Michigan State University Press, 1989.

Detweiler, Robert. *Saul Bellow: A Critical Essay.* Contemporary Writers in Christian Perspective. Grand Rapids, MI: Eerdmans, 1967.

Dutton, Robert R. *Saul Bellow,* revised edition. Twayne's United States Author Series. Boston: Twayne Publishers, 1982.

Glenday, Michael K. *Saul Bellow and the Decline of Humanism.* London: Macmillan, 1990.

Harris, Mark. *Saul Bellow: Drumlin Woodchuck.* Athens: University of Georgia Press, 1980.

Hyland, Peter. *Saul Bellow.* Modern Novelists. London: Macmillan, 1992.

Kiernan, Robert F. *Saul Bellow.* New York: Continuum, 1989.

Kulshreshta, Chirantan. *Saul Bellow: The Problem of Affirmation.* New Delhi: Arnold, 1978.

Malin, Irving. *Saul Bellow's Fiction.* Crosscurrents/Modern Critiques. Carbondale: Southern Illinois University Press, 1969.

McCadden, Joseph F. *The Flight From Women in the Fiction of Saul Bellow.* Washington, DC: University Press of America, 1981.

Newman, Judie. *Saul Bellow and History.* New York: St. Martin's Press, 1984.

Opdahl, Keith M. *The Novels of Saul Bellow: An Introduction.* University Park: Pennsylvania State University Press, 1967.

Selected Bibliography

Pifer, Ellen. *Saul Bellow Against the Grain*. Philadelphia: University of Pennsylvania Press, 1990.

Porter, M. Gilbert. *Whence the Power?: The Artistry and Humanity of Saul Bellow*. Columbia: University of Missouri Press, 1974.

Rodrigues, Eusebio L. *Quest for the Human: An Exploration of Saul Bellow's Fiction*. Lewisburg, PA: Bucknell University Press, 1981.

Rovit, Earl. *Saul Bellow*. University of Minnesota Pamphlets on American Writers 65. Minneapolis: University of Minnesota Press, 1967.

Scheer-Schaezler, Brigitte. *Saul Bellow*. Modern Literature Monographs. New York: Ungar, 1972.

Stout, Janis P. "Suffering as Meaning in Saul Bellow's *Seize the Day*," *Renascence* 39 (1987), 365–73.

Tanner, Tony. *Saul Bellow*. Edinburgh and London: Oliver and Boyd, 1965.

Wilson, Jonathan. *On Bellow's Planet: Readings From the Dark Side*. Rutherford, NJ: Fairleigh Dickinson University Press, 1985.

129

.